Calligraphy

© 2012 Kerswell Farm Ltd

This edition published by King Books

Printed 2012

This book is distributed in the UK by
Parkham Books Ltd
Barns Farm, Boraston
Tenbury Wells
Worcestershire
WR15 8NB

david@kingbooks.co.uk

ISBN: 978-1-906239-81-7

DS0257. Calligraphy

Creative Director: Sarah King
Project Editor: Sally MacEachern
Designer: Jade Sienkiewicz
Photography: Paul Forrester

This material is a selection from *Calligraphy - beginner's art guide*

Printed in Singapore

1 3 5 7 9 10 8 6 4 2

Calligraphy

MARIE LYNSKEY

Contents

Introduction

Mass-produced and quickly discarded things have become commonplace in our lives today, with the result that handwritten and hand-painted documents that have been created with more thought, time and attention have become increasingly precious and worthy of a place in our busy lives. Because the printed word on the page or computer screen is forever before us, it is a refreshing change and a great satisfaction to those who appreciate their value to be able to produce and view decorative lettering that has been prepared with time and care simply for the pleasure that it gives.

The history of writing

We can trace the history of writing back to ancient times, to the cuneiform script of the Sumerians over 5,000 years ago. Clay tablets were used, the images being pressed into the damp clay, which was then baked hard. Many tablets of this sort have been discovered (fig. 1).

The word cuneiform actually means 'wedge-shaped', as the tools employed for making the information impressed the clay with small, wedge-shaped marks, tapering from a wide start to a thin, pointed end. The earliest images were attempts to describe pictorially the information that the writer was trying to convey, but a more contained selection of symbols gradually came to be adopted, which represented spoken sounds rather than things. Although this set of symbols was eventually reduced in number as the centuries went by, it was still far from reaching today's alphabet of 26 letters. The cuneiform script spread with the conquering of Sumeria by the Babylonians, who in turn were overtaken by the Assyrians. The script was adopted by conquering peoples and was dispersed by fleeing native peoples, causing it to spread throughout the Middle East.

The Egyptians were developing their writing skills at the same time as the Sumerians, but they advanced further by developing a smaller series of symbols. Their hieroglyphics (the word means 'sacred engraved writing') were essentially picture-writing systems, and the use of a reed brush or pen and papyrus made the task simpler than the Sumerians' clay tablets (fig.2). Egyptian scribes used black ink made from carbon mixed with water and gum and red ink made with a natural, red earth pigment mixed in the same way.

Papyrus is made from the pith of reeds grown in Egypt; it is kept in rolls and is only written upon on one side, the other not being suitable for lettering (fig. 3). Papyrus is constructed by removing the outer covering of the papyrus reed and cutting the inner pith into thin layers. These strips are laid side by side lengthways, with the edges overlapping slightly. A second layer of strips is placed on top, at right angles to the first row. Next the layers are

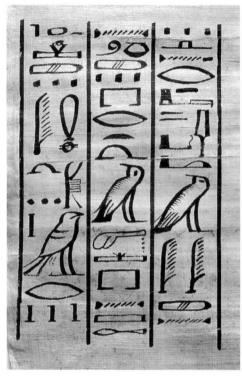

fig.2. Reconstructed hieroglyphics on papyrus.

fig. 1. Reconstruction of cuneiform lettering on clay tablet.

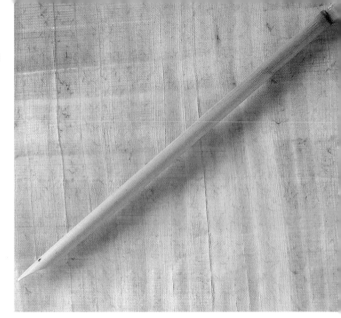

fig. 3. Papyrus, made of overlapping strips of papyrus reed and reed pen.

beaten flat, to remove some of the moisture. The papyrus is then left to dry under pressure in order to keep it flat and smooth, and the natural adhesive in the plant binds the strips together to form a single sheet.

The Egyptians clung to their pictorial writing long after some of their neighbours had begun to devise more efficient writing systems that consisted of fewer symbols. The Phoenicians adopted a style that owed its beginnings to both cuneiform and hieroglyphics, developing an alphabet that contained a similar number of letters to those that we now use (fig. 4).

It is from them that the Greeks may have developed their writing techniques, adapting the Phoenician letters and incorporating signs to represent their own sounds. The angular letters of some Greek lettering styles (fig.5) may have been due to the use of a wax tablet; it is easier to form straight lines when writing in wax with an iron or wooden stylus. The wax tablet was a wooden tray with a small lip round the edge and a coating of a thin layer of wax over the inner surface. Once the tablet was written upon, the letters could be easily erased by slightly melting and then smoothing out the wax again.

Calligraphy

fig. 4 Phoenician letters.

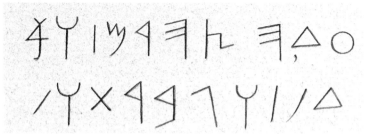

*A*s papyrus became more expensive and difficult to obtain as a result of the deterioration of the Mediterranean trade routes and Rome's decline in power, vellum and parchment began to replace it. Vellum is the specially prepared skin of calves or goats, while parchment is the skin of sheep. The surface of both is very smooth and easy to write upon, and the sheets could either be white or cream, with slight, but attractive, vein markings running through the skins. Leather had been used as a writing surface by Hebrew scribes, who wrote from right to left, and it is thought that vellum was first produced in Pergamum in Asia Minor (the German word for vellum is Pergament, which seems to bear out this theory).

Roman lettering followed on from the Greek, and the Latin alphabets varied from very precisely drawn capitals, such as the quadrata, or square-capital, alphabet that was carved on stone (fig. 6), to such more free-flowing, quickly written styles as rustica (fig. 7), which was used in documents. These styles spread throughout the Roman Empire. Vellum furthermore brought about the construction of books, whereas papyrus had been rolled up.

fig. 5. Greek letters.

The quill pen was also devised and became a well-used writing instrument. Quills are much more flexible than reed pens, and as a consequence the styles that were written with them evolved accordingly (see p24 for instructions on making your own quill pen).

Arabic scripts were also derived from the Phoenicians' system, culminating in the writing of the Koran, which standardised the script during the early seventh century. It spread rapidly throughout the regions that were conquered by the Arabs, but its spread towards Western Europe was halted by Arab defeats at the hands of the Franks. Some of the earliest writing on vellum is Arabic (fig. 8).

Chinese lettering dates from at least 1000 bc, and developed in much the same way as cuneiform, using picture forms, but in vertical columns – indeed, it still follows this method (fig. 9). We are indebted to the Chinese for their invention of paper in about ad 100 (they had previously used wood, bamboo and silk as writing surfaces, but paper came to be regarded the most practical material). Its use gradually spread, first to Japan and eventually towards the West, progressing via the Islamic countries to Spain and the rest of Europe. One of the earliest-known European manuscripts to have been written on paper is a deed of King Roger of Sicily dated 1109, whose text is written in both Arabic and Greek. Paper was being used in England from the mid-thirteenth century, but paper manufacture did not begin in this country until the end of the fifteenth century, when a small

fig. 6. Quadrata capitals.

fig. 7. Rustica capitals.

fig. 8. Arabic writing on vellum.

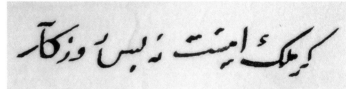

paper mill was set up in Hertfordshire by John Tate. Another two centuries would pass before its use became widespread and it supplanted vellum as the principal writing surface.

The development of lettering styles in Europe

Returning to late Roman lettering, a script known as uncial was developed and used in Roman books (fig.10), which later became the script of the Celtic monasteries as missionaries dispersed throughout Europe spreading Christianity, which had become the official religion of Rome during the fourth century. The Romans wrote on vellum with quill pens, and it was possible to achieve a much finer quality of letter with these precisely cut writing instruments.

With the break up of the Roman Empire during the fifth century, widespread communications deteriorated and it was largely the Roman Catholic Church that kept arts and learning alive throughout the Dark Ages. The uncial script was adopted by Christian scribes and became the dominant book hand in the West from the fifth to eighth centuries. Christians required texts that explained their religion to enable them to spread their message, and the Greek word biblos describes their primary book, or Bible, which was copied, re-copied and illuminated on an ever-increasing scale. The production of Christian illuminated manuscripts thrived in isolated parts of Europe, and the seventh and eighth centuries saw the creation of some of the most complex and attractive manuscripts ever produced in what became known as the insular style. Missionaries and monks took books with them on their travels and thus encouraged the spread of different lettering styles throughout Europe. The books were lent and copied (this was the only means of acquiring a new book), and many medieval manuscripts depict monks at work, their writing materials and paints being clearly visible.

Although the uncial alphabet consisted of majuscule (capital) letters, a minuscule (small) alphabet was also beginning to emerge. The uncial hand deteriorated towards the ninth century, its spacious-ness and formality being replaced by a more quickly written and economically spaced style. A mix-ture of the formal uncial that was used in great works and the more cursive versions that were used in informal writings gradually came to be known as the half-uncial script (fig.11).

*T*he next major style was developed as a result of the Holy Roman Emperor Charlemagne's wish to promote learning. Charlemagne, the king of the Franks who lived from 742 to 814, gave his name

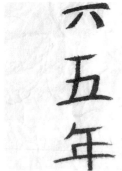

fig. 9. Chinese lettering.

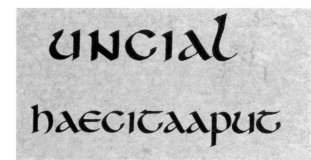

fig. 10. Uncial letters.

Calligraphy

halɟ uncial
nobiſ cunae ɟuið

fig. 11. Half uncial letters.

to the Carolingian script (fig.12), which had long ascending and descending stokes to the letters and a free-flowing, elegant style. Charlemagne's patronage of the arts brought about the widespread adoption of minuscule alphabets, and we can trace the formation of a series of closely related styles throughout Europe.

In France, there was the Merovingian style (fig.13), which was named after the dynasty which preceded Charlemagne's. An insular style of lettering (fig.14) continued to develop in northern Britain and was not superseded by the Carolingian until the mid-tenth century. Anglo-Saxon lettering (fig.15), which was influenced by Roman missionaries, was introduced by monks from England to continental Europe.

The Spanish Visigothic (fig.16) was a style that survived into the twelfth century, while the Beneventan script(fig.17) evolved in Monte Cassino in southern Italy during the ninth century and survived into the thirteenth century. All of these lettering styles thrived in Europe, and were used in the manuscripts that were produced in various centres of learning throughout the early Middle Ages.

*T*he thirteenth century saw the emergence of the Gothic scripts (fig.18), whereby the rounded letter shapes that had been used during the previous centuries became gradually more angular, culminating in the textura script (fig.19) of the fourteenth century, with its dense, black covering of vertical lines connected by thin, hairline strokes. Richly decorated Gothic manuscripts, illuminated with gold leaf and reflecting the extravagant fashions, courtly life and romantic ideals that were popular at the time, were produced for great patrons of the arts. In Italy, the rotunda style (fig.20), which represented a return to a more rounded version of the Gothic hand, found favour, particularly in music books. The Gothic styles took up much less space than the Carolingian hands, which enabled more text to be fitted into a page. Gothic was the first lettering style to appear in the printed books that were first produced during the fifteenth century. As a result, slowly produced, handwritten books began to decline in numbers, while increasingly widely available printed books carried the written word to classes of people who had never before had the chance to possess it. An attractive style known as bastarda (fig.21) bridged the gap to the next major changes in lettering styles that were brought about by the Renaissance. Bastarda was a cursive amalgamation and adaptation of the Gothic and Carolingian styles that appeared in Europe during the fifteenth century. The letters are quite curved, but with angular points at the top and bottom. Although it was adapted as an informal writing style, some beautiful formal examples can be found in the form of official documents and poetry, although not religious documents.

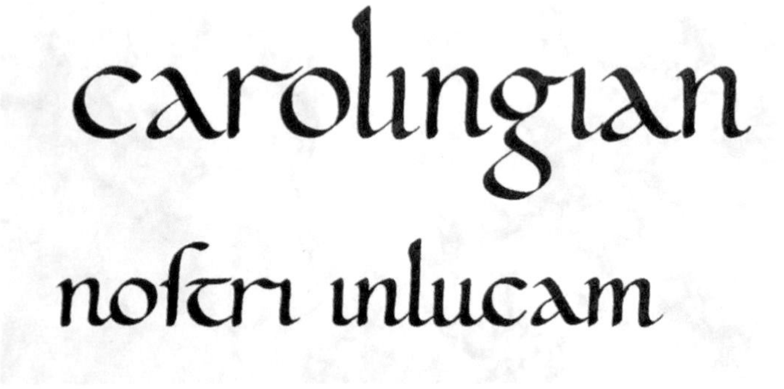

fig. 12. Carolingian letters.

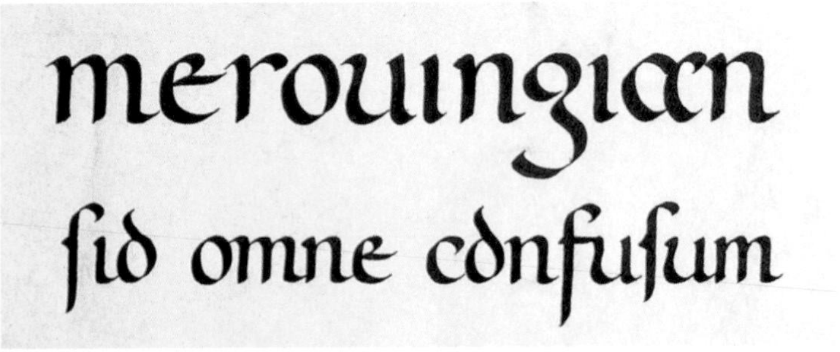

carolingian

nofcri inlucam

fig. 13. Merovingian letters.

merouingian

fid omne cdnfufum

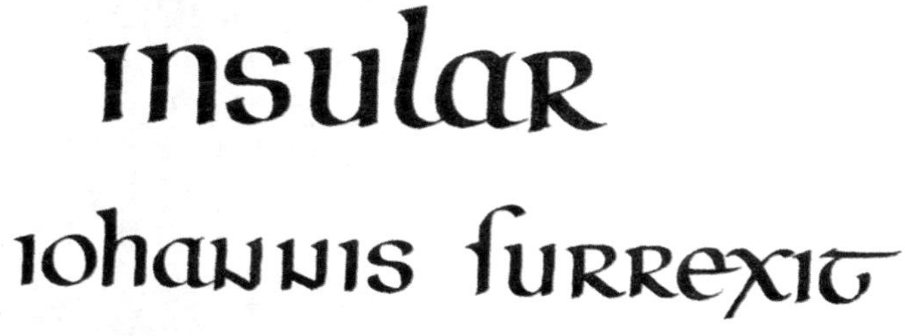

insular

iohannis furrexit

fig. 14. Insular letters.

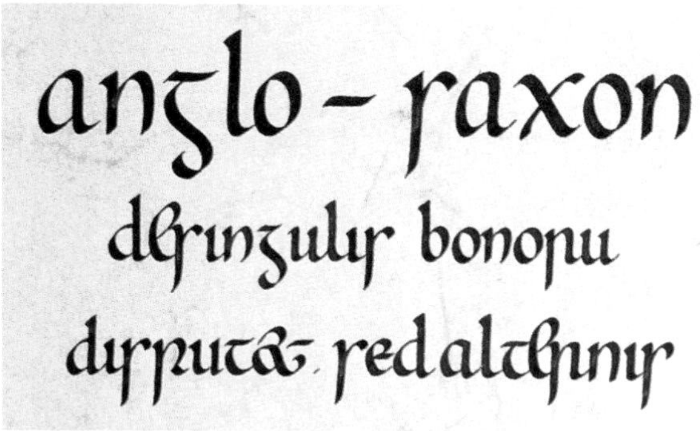

anglo - raxon

dchinzulir bonopu
dyrputæ; red alchinir

fig. 15. Anglo-saxon letters.

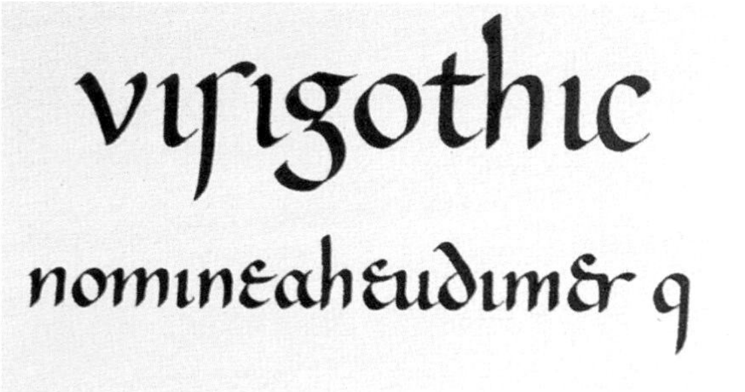

visigothic

nomineahtudimer q

fig. 16. Visigothic letters.

beneventan

quiæ læm nonptopæ

fig.17. Beneventan letters.

*I*taly spearheaded the introduction of the Renaissance lettering styles, which represented attempts by scholars to return to the simpler styles that had preceded the Gothic scripts. Such styles as the Carolingian were used as models, but the new styles had a gradual tendency to slope to the right and to become increasingly cursive, no doubt in the interests of speed. This italic hand, as it became known, soon became very popular and widespread. Cancelleresca, which had a neat, formal appearance, was one form of italic script that emerged (fig.22), while another, the humanistic hand (fig.23), had a neat, clear-cut precision to its letters and evolved as a result of the study of antiquarian Roman styles.

With the widespread production of printed books, we finally arrive at the copperplate style (fig.24), which was first formed by the action of the engraver's burin – an engraving tool with a sharp point – on printing plates. Interestingly, the terms 'lower case', which is often applied to minuscule letters, and 'upper case', which describes majuscule or capital letters, are derived from the cases, or drawers, in which printers kept their different sets of type. Copperplate came to be used to form fantastically flourished lettering, sometimes embellished almost to the point of illegibility. When written with a fine-pointed pen and ink, the letters could be very beautiful, and it was the copperplate script that filled the copybooks that many writing masters used to teach handwriting. From the beginning of the nineteenth century, steel pens began to be produced and manufactured in quantity; these had the advantage over quill pens of ease of acquisition and greater durability and consequently became widely used.

fig. 18. Gothic letters.

gothic
Op fyŋ houet

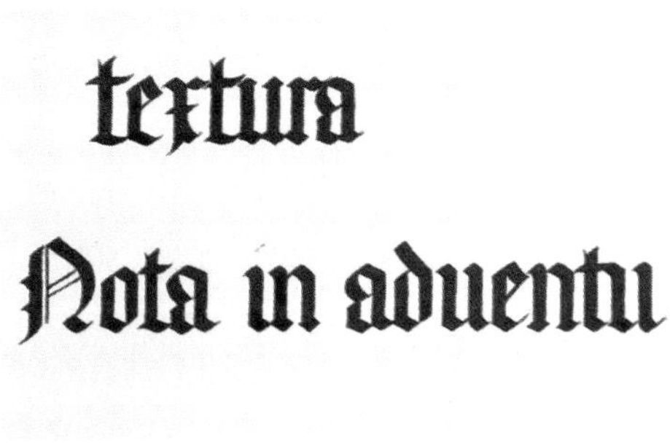

textura

Nota in aduentu

fig. 19. Textura letters.

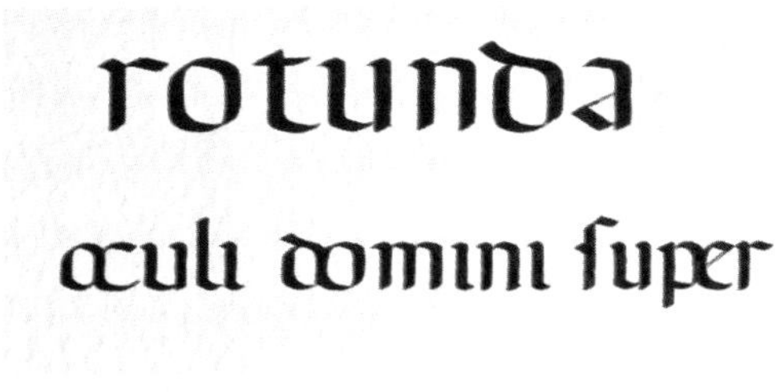

rotunda

oculi domini super

fig. 20. Rotunda letters.

bastarda

deus miseratur

fig. 21. Bastarda letters.

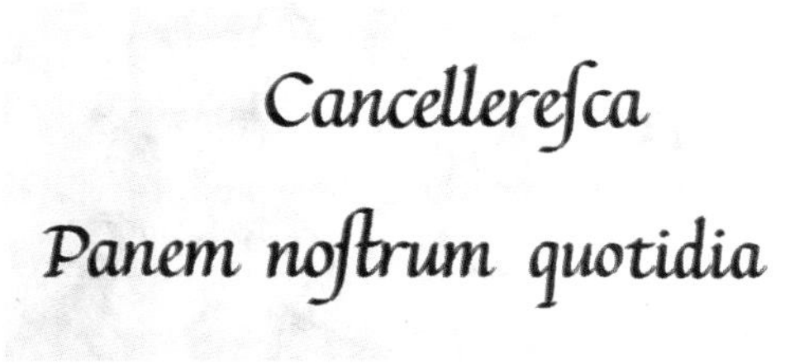

Cancelleresca

Panem nostrum quotidia

fig.22. Cancelleresca letters.

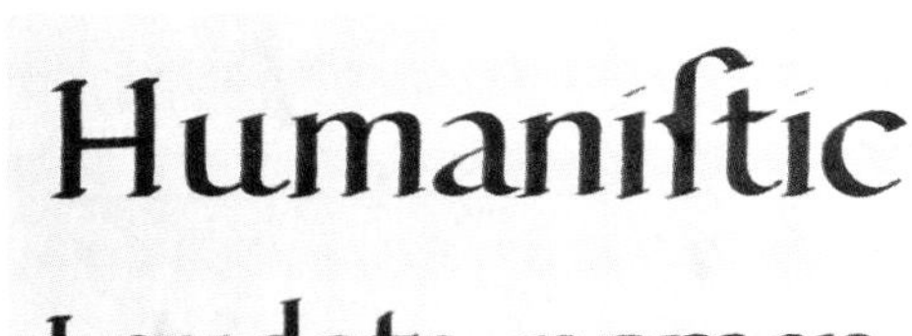

Humanistic

Laudate nomen

fig. 23. Humanistic letters.

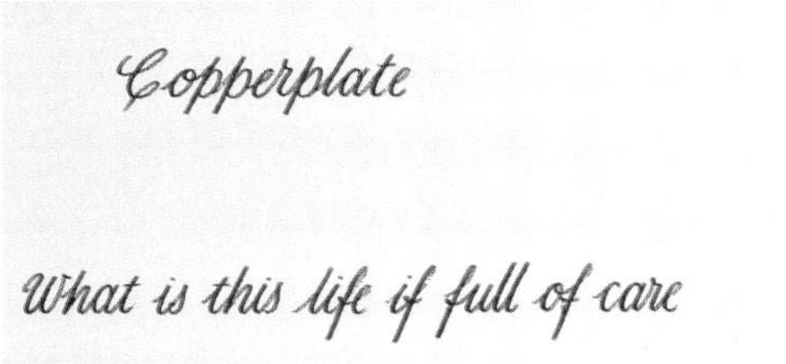

Copperplate

What is this life if full of care
we have no time to stand and stare

fig. 24. Copperplate letters.

1

Materials and equipment

Materials and equipment for the scribe

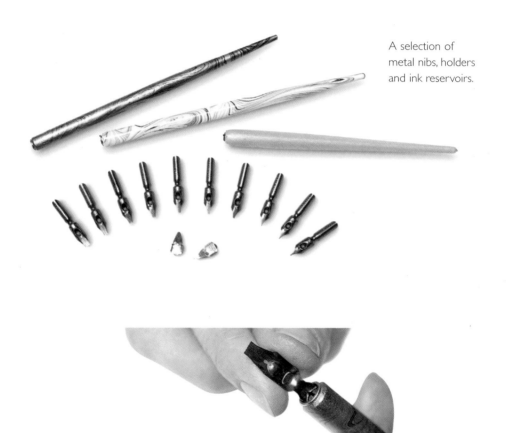

A selection of metal nibs, holders and ink reservoirs.

fig.1. Attaching the nib to the penholder.

Calligraphy, or the study and reproduction of historical lettering styles, as well as the creation of new lettering styles, is today a very popular recreational activity. The array of materials and equipment that is now available to the scribe and illuminator is both very wide and varied in quality. The equipment and materials that you will need at the outset are discussed below.

Pens and nibs

Although metal nibs have been in use since Roman times, early examples were not very satisfactory. Now produced by many different manufacturers, good metal nibs can produce excellent results. It is important that you use proper calligraphy pens and nibs if you want to create really good lettering. Fountain pens may be easy to use, but their nibs are never sharp enough to produce distinctly contrasting thin-and-thick strokes, and it is these that give most calligraphic hands their style and beauty. Nibs come in a wide variety of styles and sizes. For consistency, William Mitchell nibs have been used throughout this book. They are one of the best brands to use. If you buy other brands you may find that sizes vary. A size 70 for one brand may be another brand's size 0.

A calligraphic pen consists of a nib-holder, a nib and a small reservoir to hold the ink. The nib is first fitted into the holder (fig.1), and the reservoir fitted last (fig. 2).

After gaining some initial experience with metal nibs, it is well worth trying quills and reed pens in order to widen your understanding of calligraphy and your ability. If you cannot make your own quill pen, you may be able to buy a ready-made one; because demand is small, however, they may be difficult to find. If this is the case, try contacting a local or national lettering society to ask if they know of a supplier or can put you in touch with a scribe who will make pens for you.

A homemade quill pen
Curing a quill

A quill pen is made from the feather of a large bird, such as a goose or swan. One of the first five flight feathers is used, as these are the largest and strongest (fig. 3).

A quill needs to be cured before it can be cut. In order to do this, you must first remove the end of the barrel and soak the feather in water for about 12 hours so that the cells expand.

fig. 2. Fitting the ink reservoir to the nib.

Remove the membrane inside the barrel with a suitable object, such as a small crochet hook or a length of wire, taking care not to scratch the barrel.

When it is free of obstructions, harden the barrel by plunging it into hot sand. Heat the sand (which should be as fine as possible, like the silver sand that is used by potters) in a flat pan and push the quill into the sand so that the barrel is filled. Use a spoon to scoop the sand into the quill if necessary, and leave it in the sand for only a few seconds before removing it to examine it. The opaque, white colour of the barrel should have become transparent, and provided that there is no distortion or blistering to the quill from overheating you can continue to the next stage. If the quill has not been left in the sand for long enough it will be too pliable when it cools, so it will probably be necessary for you to learn by trial and error when the quill has become hard enough to write with, but not so hard as to be brittle when it is cut.

Shake out the sand. While the quill is still hot and slightly pliable, scrape off the membrane from the outside of the barrel with a blunt knife in order to avoid scratching it. Then dip it into cold water and dry it in order to prepare it for cutting (fig. 4).

Shorten the feather to a length of no more than about 20 to 25cm (8 to 10") and remove the plume from both sides of the quill. Alternatively, if you prefer to keep a little plume for appearance's sake, you can leave some on the side which will not rest against your hand, although you will find it less cumbersome if you trim this down to about 1cm (½") in width. All of the barb (the plumage around the top end of the quill) must be removed, as it would otherwise interfere with your hand when writing.

Calligraphy

fig. 3. An untreated quill.　　　　　　　　　　　　　　fig. 4. A cured quill.

Ink

The type of ink that you use is very important, as it is difficult to produce good letters with a poor-quality ink. There are many bottled inks on the market, ranging from thin, transparent liquids, which often flow very blotchily from the pen and are likely to fade when exposed to daylight for long periods, to quite acceptable, strong blacks that have the correct consistency. It is worth experimenting with various types of ink so that you get an idea of what is available and which ink is the most suitable for you.

Chinese ink

The best ink is Chinese ink, which will not fade when exposed to strong sunlight. Although it can be bought in liquid form in bottles, solid sticks of ink which are ground in an ink slate (fig.6) produce the highest-quality ink. The sharpness of letter that can be achieved with Chinese ink sticks is infinitely superior to that produced by bottled inks.

fig. 6. Chinese Ink stick and slate.

*F*ill the deep end of the slate with enough water to make the quantity of liquid ink that you think you will need. The ink must be freshly ground on the day that you intend to use it because it thickens and goes off if it is kept for too long. It is therefore usually only necessary to grind up a small amount at a time.

Making your quill pen

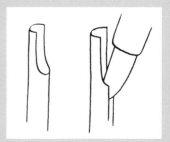

1 First remove the end of the barrel, then cure as detailed previously.

2 Using a very sharp knife, remove the end of the barrel, cutting along a long, slanting angle.

3 Make a short slit down the length of the quill. Work carefully, and lever the blade gently, until the quill cracks to form the slit.

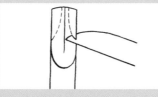

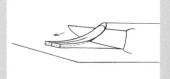

4 Next cut a large scoop out of the opposite side to the slit, so that the slit is more or less centred in the remaining portion. This cut is quite difficult, and you will probably have to try several quills before you produce a good pen.

5 Make a cut on each side of the slit to form the writing edge. Make sure that you match each side so that the slit is central and the pen is of the required width.

6 To make the writing edge clean and sharp, rest the end of the quill on a smooth, hard surface and thin the tip slightly with a forward stroke.

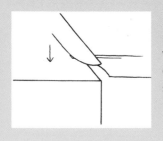

7 Finally, remove a tiny portion from the tip with a downward cut to create a completely straight edge.

The pen should now be ready (fig.5), but dip it in ink and try writing a few strokes to see if it is smooth and well cut. The end of the nib can be re-cut if it is not correct or after it has become blunt through use.

Calligraphy

Grind the ink stick back and forth along the full length of the slate, taking the water with it until a very strong, black ink is produced. You will need to apply heavy pressure and will probably have to grind the stick for at least 15 minutes.

During the grinding process, keep testing the strength of the ink by painting a little on a sheet of paper to see if it is dark enough when it dries. When you are happy with the appearance of the ink, apply it to the pen with a small brush (fig.7).

fig. 7. Applying ink to the nib with a brush.

fig. 5. The completed quill pen.

Paper

Good-quality cartridge paper is ideal when you start to practise calligraphy. It is worth buying a pad of A2-sized (596 x 422mm) paper from an art shop, because the practice lettering that you will begin with will be quite large, and you will therefore need to work on large sheets of paper if you are to fit a reasonable number of lines of lettering onto the page.

*A*void paper which is on the thin side, however, as it will crinkle up when the ink makes it wet. Some papers are also too shiny to take ink very well, and you will either find that your letters are not sharp enough or that the ink sits on the surface of the paper and takes too long to dry. Try to find cartridge paper of about 120gsm (grammes per square metre), which should have the right weight and surface quality for your lettering. (See Chapter 7 for different types of paper and a little more on their manufacture.)

Drawing boards

It is vital that you write on a sloping surface so that the pen meets the paper at the most advantageous angle. When you first take up calligraphy, you can make do with a board – perhaps a piece of fibreboard measuring about 60 by 90cm (2 by 3') from a DIY store – resting against a table and on your lap (fig.8). As you progress, however, you will find it more convenient to acquire a small drawing board, which you can set up at a fixed angle (fig.9). You can buy good drawing boards from well-equipped art shops, and some have a parallel rule attached that can save you a lot of time when ruling up sheets of paper (fig.10).

*F*ixing a few sheets of blotting paper to the surface of the drawing board is an important modification that will enable you to write on a slightly springy surface rather than a hard, flat one. Try to find large sheets of blotting paper that will cover a reasonably large area and fix two sheets to the board with masking tape (fig.11).

A guard sheet is the next requirement, and this should be as long as your board will allow, as you will need to move the paper underneath it from side to side as you work along each line of text. The positioning of the guard sheet is important: you should find the most comfortable position for writing at your board while also ensuring that your eye level is as shown in fig.12. Attach the guard sheet in such a way that the line of lettering that you will be working on appears at the correct level.

As you write, make sure that your hands always rest on the guard sheet and not on the paper that you are writing on. This is very important advice, as no matter how clean you believe your hands to be, they will always deposit small amounts of grease on the paper that they touch. This can have dire consequences for your work, because greasy paper will not absorb ink well and you will produce poor-quality letters if you write over any greasy patches.

The calligraphic styles in this book

Having gathered all of the equipment and materials that you will need, you are ready to proceed. The lettering styles illustrated in this beginner's manual are adaptations of some of the historical examples detailed above that have been modified in the interests of clarity, consistency and ease of production. Together they constitute an interesting range of hands that are suitable for a wide variety of uses and occasions.

fig. 8. Drawing board resting on lap and table.

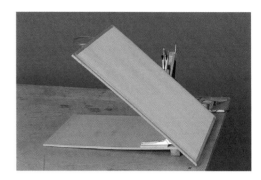

fig. 9. Small portable drawing board.

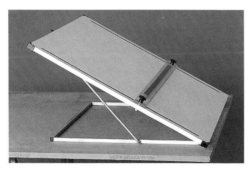

fig. 10. Large drawing board with parallel rule.

fig. 11. Add blotting paper to the board.

fig. 12. Add guard sheet at correct level for writing height.

2

Foundation- hand lettering

Foundation-hand lettering

When you write formal lettering, one of the first things that you have to consider is the size of your nib in relation to the writing lines that you are going to use. It is always best to start writing between top and bottom guidelines to enable you to make straight, even lines of lettering. Some people like to dispense with the guidelines after a short time, but using them is far more reliable, and it doesn't take much time to draw up sets of pencilled guidelines that can be rubbed out later.

Ruling writing lines

Writing lines that are five times the width of the nib are appropriate for most lettering styles, and when you begin you should use a fairly large nib, such as the size 1½ William Mitchell nib, which is about 2.5mm (³⁄₃₂") in width. You can determine the width of your writing lines by making a series of five small strokes, side by side, with your pen (fig.1), which will give you the correct width. You should then rule up a sheet of paper with sets of writing lines. Allow twice the width of the writing lines between each pair of lines to give enough space for the ascending and descending strokes (fig. 2).

Regulating the ink flow

Before tackling the foundation-hand alphabet shown in fig. 4, begin by gaining some experience in using your pen by drawing the various strokes that you can make with it. Dipping the whole nib into the ink tends to be rather messy and leaves a lot of surplus ink outside the space between

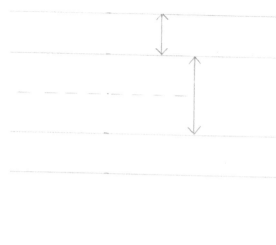

fig. 1. Five nib widths are used to determine the height of the writing lines.

fig. 2. Ruling up a page of writing lines.

the nib and reservoir, which is the part of the pen that actually delivers the ink to the edge of the nib and thus transfers it to the page. Instead, fill the nib with ink by applying the ink with a small brush and drawing it across the opening between the reservoir and the nib so that the ink fills most of the gap (see fig. 7, page 25).

Start by making some diagonal lines following the direction of the pen (fig. 3), so that the stroke is as broad as the width of the nib. Try to make the ink flow freely and evenly from the whole width of the nib, without leaving any gaps or making any scratches. If you have trouble getting the ink to flow from the pen, you may have positioned the reservoir against the nib too tightly, thereby preventing

the ink from flowing through. Reservoirs vary slightly in their manufacture, and some can be a little tight. If you think that this could be the problem, bend back the tip of the reservoir slightly. The side wings can also be adjusted either outwards or inwards if the reservoir is too tight or too loose.

Another reason why the ink may not be coming out is that the reservoir tip is too far away from the end of the nib. Finally, you may have applied too little ink to the nib so that it is not reaching the writing edge. If you have the reverse problem – too much ink flowing from the pen – then you should either adjust the reservoir so that there is less of a gap between the reservoir and nib or else move the point of the reservoir a little further from the writing edge.

fig.3. Diagonal practice strokes.

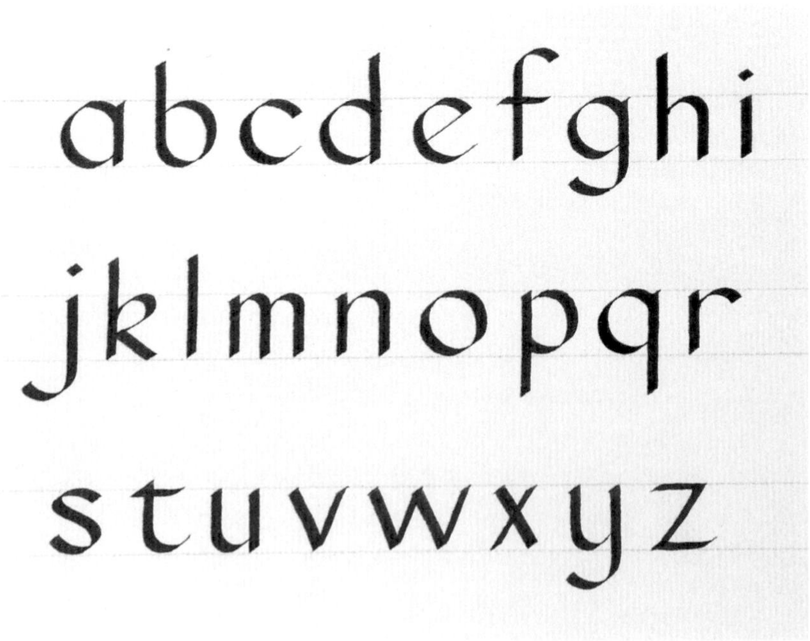

fig.4. The foundation-hand alphabet.

abcdefghi
jklmnopqr
stuvwxyz

Experimenting with strokes

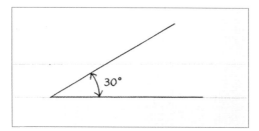

1 The angle at which you hold the pen should be about 30° to the paper.

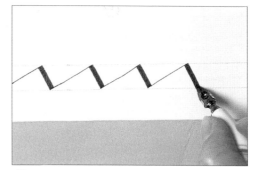

2 When the ink is running smoothly from the pen and your diagonal lines are even, with no jagged edges, try making a zigzag pattern. You are now making the thickest and thinnest lines that the pen can produce, and the nib should be moving from side to side for the thin strokes and in a straight line for the broad strokes. Note that if the correct, 30° angle is maintained, the thin stroke will always be longer than the broad stroke.

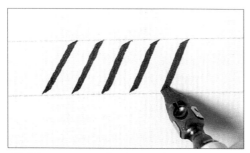

3 Next try some backward-sloping diagonals, which are slightly more difficult to produce. Try to reproduce the same angle and thickness of the strokes shown, as these are written with the pen held at the correct angle.

4 Keeping the pen at 30°, carefully make these strokes and then practise crosses, keeping both parts of the cross well-balanced.

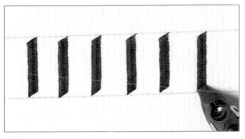

5 Now try some vertical lines taking care to keep the strokes as upright as possible. If one edge is jagged and the other smooth, you are probably applying too much pressure to one side. Adjust your grip and apply a little less pressure to the smooth edge and a little more to the jagged side, which should solve the problem.

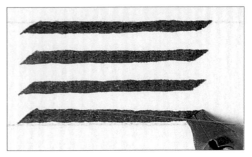

6 Practise some horizontals next. These are a little more difficult than vertical lines, as any error made along the length of the stroke tends to be more noticeable. As you gain experience in the use of your pen, however, any initial unevenness should soon disappear.

7 Curved strokes can give the novice calligrapher a lot of trouble. First, form a series of circles composed of two strokes as shown, trying to keep them as smooth and rounded as possible.

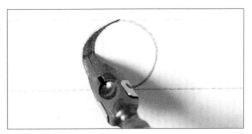

8 To start with, you could draw pencil guidelines and trace the pen around them so that you get used to the feel of the strokes when you are making them correctly. Make sure that the nib does not stray outside the pencil line.

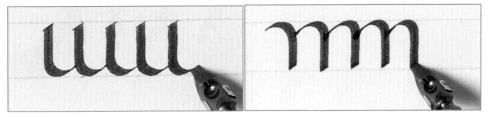

9 Next try strokes that are made up of a combination of round and straight lines.

Foundation-hand lettering

When you are ready, move on to the alphabet, here shown with directional strokes added. This is a simple style called the foundation, or round, hand, because the letters are the foundation of most other styles and are all based on a round, 'o' shape. The 'o' determines the measurement that governs the width of the other letters.

2 (see right). An 'n' is exactly the same width as the 'o', as are all of the other letters except for the 'i' and the 'l' (which are narrower because they are composed of only one stroke) and the 'm' and 'w' (which are in effect double versions of 'n' and 'v' respectively and are therefore twice the width).

3 The 'z' is the only letter for which your pen will have to make one of the strokes at a different angle. When making the central stroke of the 'z', turn the pen so that it is horizontal to the page. This produces a thicker stroke, which makes the letter look better than if it were written with the pen held at the normal angle throughout. (see below.)

Work through the letters, making the strokes in the directions shown, and then practise those that haven't worked out very well.

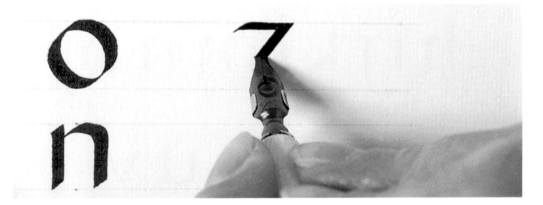

Correct spacing

*O*nce you begin to write words, you will need to think about the spacing of the letters within them. Spacing takes time to master, but after a while you will automatically find yourself judging it correctly.

The basic requirement is that the letters look in balance with each other and that none are squashed-up, or too far apart. In fig. 5 the letters are unevenly spaced and too far apart; the space between the letters is gradually widening and the letters do not look as though they all belong to the same word. In fig. 6 the letters are much too close together, giving a cramped appearance which makes the text difficult to read. In Fig. 7 the letters are correctly spaced, with as equal an amount of space as possible between each letter.

It is helpful to look on the letters as groups of three and to make sure that the central one of the three always looks as though it is exactly in the centre, and not nearer to either its left- or right-hand neighbour. In fig. 8 the first two groups of three letters are not evenly spaced. The bottom example is correct.

fig. 5. The spacing of the letters of this word is too far apart.

fig. 6. The letters are this time too close together.

fig. 8. The first two groups of three letters are not evenly spaced, the bottom example is correct.

fig. 7. The word correctly spaced.

Words that are a combination of similar types, for example, those that consist of rounded letters only, such as those in the word 'code' (fig. 9) or of straight letters only, such as in the word 'lilt' (fig.10) are much easier to space than those that contain a mixture. Words that combine both rounded and narrow letters such as 'millipede' (fig.11) are harder to balance. Here the letters are widely spaced at the beginning and closely spaced at the end.

Try to get into the habit of thinking about the space that you are leaving between each letter and always make it roughly equal. Two straight letters written side by side leave much less space between them than two rounded letters (fig.12) so they are moved further apart to give the appearance of an equal amount of space. With the less regular letters, such as 's', 'f', 'v' and 't', in which at least one side is neither completely straight nor curved, you will have to try to judge the amount of space needed to give the same effect that would be achieved with more regularly shaped letters.

The spacing between words should be about one letter's width (fig.13). If you leave too much space between words your page of lettering will appear to have too many gaps, or what are called 'rivers' of space, running down the page, in other words, the gaps between words will coincide with each other from one line to the next, forming large, blank areas on the page. By contrast, if too little space is left between words, some may look as though they are joined together.

fig. 9. A word composed mainly of rounded strokes will have the letters almost touching.

fig.10. A straight stroked word will have letters spaced well apart.

fig.11. A combination of straight and rounded strokes needs proper spacing to look correct.

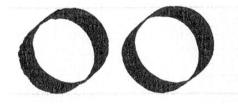

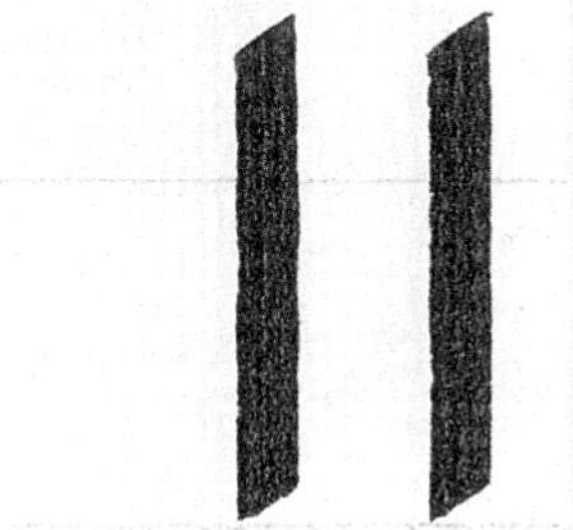

fig.12. Rounded strokes are always much closer together than straight strokes.

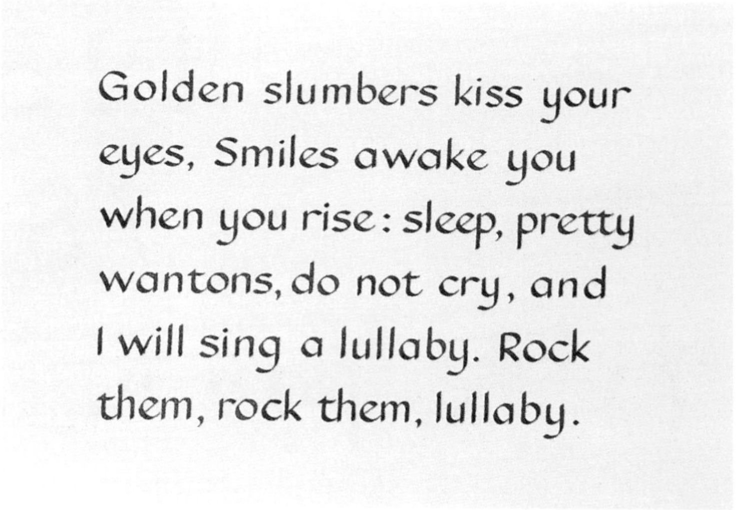

Golden slumbers kiss your eyes, Smiles awake you when you rise: sleep, pretty wantons, do not cry, and I will sing a lullaby. Rock them, rock them, lullaby.

fig.13. A gap the width of one letter is left between each word.

ABCDEF
GHIJKLM
NOPQRST
UVWXYZ

fig.14. The foundation-hand capital letters with directional strokes.

fig.15. The capital letter height is seven times the width of the nib.

Aa Bb Cc Dd

fig.16. Practise the majuscules and minuscules side by side.

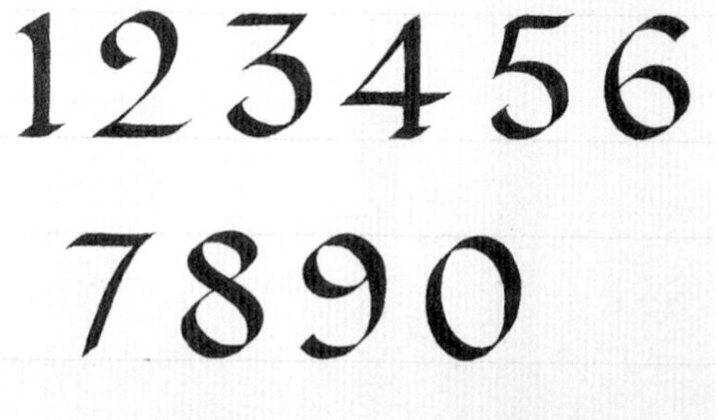

123456
7890

fig.17. Numerals.

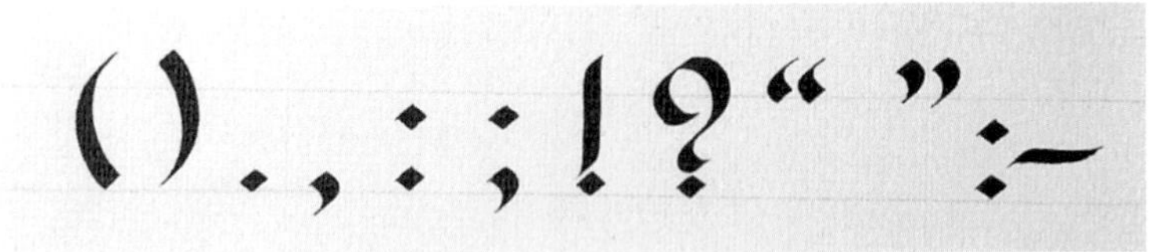

(). , : ; ! ? " " :-

fig. 18. Punctuation marks.

fig. 19. An ampersand.

*P*ractise all sorts of pieces of lettering, paying special attention to any letters that give you particular trouble or to the strokes that you find most difficult to produce. It is wise to spend a lot of time mastering the early learning stages rather than rushing into the more complex styles before you are ready.

Fig. 14 shows the foundation-hand capital, or majuscule, letters. These are written with a letter height that is seven times the width of the nib (fig. 15), so rule up a page of guidelines for these letters. After writing them in alphabetical order, practise writing groups of similarly shaped letters, such as the rounded letters 'C', 'D', 'G', 'O' and 'Q', moving on to letters that comprise vertical and horizontal strokes only, like 'E', 'F', 'H' and 'L', and then to those with diagonal strokes, such as 'T', 'K', 'V', 'W', 'X' and 'Y'. Varying the letter order like this will help you to become more familiar with the relationship of each letter to others in the alphabet.

Now write majuscule and minuscule letters together (fig. 16). Although you can work on this practice piece using guidelines for the five- and seven-nib-width measurements to ensure that you make the capitals the correct height, you would normally only use the height required for the minuscule letters, and would judge the capitals by eye.

In order to write a piece of lettering containing the correct grammar, you will need to insert punctuation marks (fig. 18), and numerals (fig. 17). Although the brackets, exclamation mark and question mark are all drawn at capital-letter height, the colon and semi-colon look best when they are written with their top marks just below the top minuscule writing line. An ampersand is shown in fig. 19

Adding serifs

*T*he plain letters of the foundation hand are improved and linked with small strokes known as serifs. The various types of serif are constructed as shown in fig. 20. The full serifed alphabet is shown in fig. 21, and the serifed capital letters are shown in fig. 22.

The serif at the top of ascending strokes and at the beginning of most of the capital letters starts with a thin stroke drawn from right to left and then traces an arching curve back to the right again. Now make the upright stroke so that it falls in line with the curving stroke. Do not make the first two strokes too long, or you will leave a small gap in the centre of the three strokes and the serif will be too large. These two strokes really only need to be the equivalent of one nib width to produce the correct-sized serif.

The serifs at the foot of the 'f', 'p' and 'q', as well as many of the feet of the capital letters, are made by taking the pen to the left, just short of the point at which the letter will finish, and then making a horizontal stroke that cuts across the upright without leaving a gap. The other serifs are less complicated, being just a slight curve at the beginning or end of a stroke.

The 'm' is a good example of a letter that needs a mixture of slightly different serifs in order to make it look well balanced. The first serif at the beginning of the first vertical is a smaller curve than those that will make up the next two strokes. At the feet of the first and second verticals are small serifs that turn slightly towards the right. The final serif can be a little more pronounced. If this larger serif were used for the first two strokes, it would fill too much of the gap between the vertical strokes and would mar the legibility of the letter.

The cross strokes of the 'f', 't' and 'z' can just be given a slight turn at either end to add a smooth flow to the letter and to take away the hard, plain look of the unserifed stroke.

It is not necessary – and, indeed, is sometimes even a mistake – to try to join up the letters with too many serifs. Serifs should be simple adornments that give a more pleasing appearance to the text and do not detract from its clarity and legibility. Overdone serifs can really spoil the look of the lettering (fig. 23) and can also make it difficult to read. The 'r' is the letter that is mistreated more than any other in this way (fig. 24), and when forming it try not to give the foot of the downstroke more than a slight turn, or it will end up looking more like a badly formed 'c'.

When changing to different lettering sizes, remember to make your writing lines five times the width of the nib. Avoid sizes below the William Mitchell No 3 nib, which is about 1.25mm (³⁄₃₂") in width, at this stage, because smaller lettering is more difficult. Although it can hide errors, it is better to learn to form the letters correctly from the outset. Fig. 25 illustrates writing lines for lettering drawn with a size 3 and a size 2 Mitchell nib.

Calligraphy

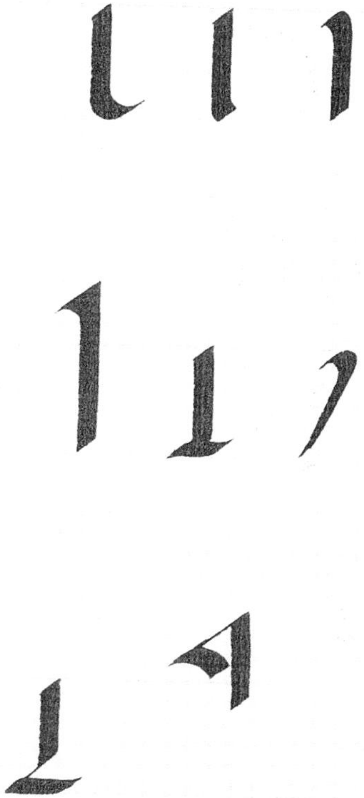

fig. 20. Types of serif: the first three examples are simple curves completing some of the upright strokes; the following two are composed of two strokes, as shown underneath – a narrow stroke to the left and then the broad stroke completing the serif; the remaining example is a diagonal stroke which finishes with a smooth curve.

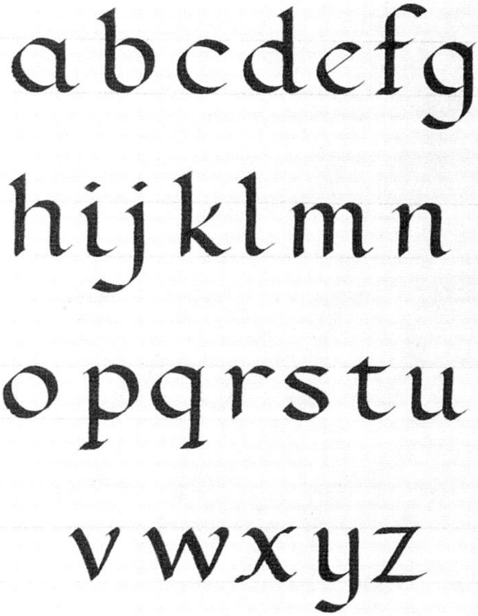

abcdefg
hijklmn
opqrstu
vwxyz

fig. 21. The foundation-hand alphabet with serifs.

ABCDEFG
HIJKLMN
OPQRSTU
VWXYZ

fig. 22. Serifed foundation-hand capitals.

r r

fig. 23. The foot of the 'r' is frequently given too large a curve. The correct 'r' is on the left.

race

fig. 24. Here the correctly written word is shown above.

race

Calligraphy

fig. 25. Writing lines for nib sizes 2 and 3.

Pen patterns

Pen patterns are not
only good fun to produce,
but cn also be extremely
useful for embellishin small
calligraphy projects. There is
no end to the attractive
patterns that you can make,
and fig. 26. shows a selection.
Practise reproducing them.

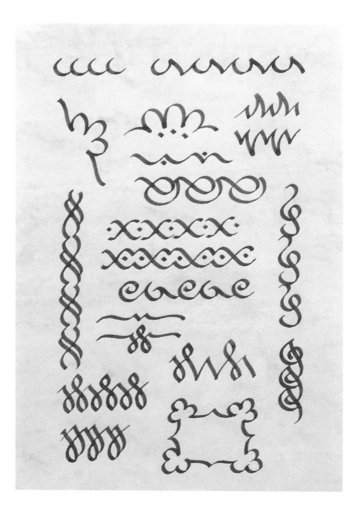

fig. 26. Pen patterns.

Making simple labels

*I*n order to practise and make use of what you have learned so far, you could use the foundation hand to make a few labels for home produce.

Raspberry

1 On your chosen paper, write the main words that will be contained on the label in a large lettering size. Leave plenty of space around the words so that you can trim the label to size.

25th August

2 Write the secondary information in a smaller size on a separate practice sheet. Measure the amount of space that the text takes up and mark this length on the label under the first line.

Raspberry Jam

3 Rule the writing lines for the smaller lettering and mark the width so that it will be centralised beneath the main lettering.

Raspberry Jam

25th August 2000

4 Write the secondary information within the marked space, making sure it is centred below the first line.

5 Draw a pen pattern around the edge as a little embellishment.

6 You could also add a small line drawing to decorate the label further.

7 Calligraphic line drawings are easy to do: first make a pencil sketch of your subject and then work out the direction of the strokes that will be needed to form a nicely shaped picture. When you have found the best way in which to create the picture, repeat the process on the label.

8 Any fruit shape can be pen drawn with a little care.

As an alternative to the horizontally laid out label above, you can follow the same basic steps to create a vertical, or portrait style label, as shown here.

3

Italic lettering

Italic lettering

We will now move on to italic lettering, which is basically the same as the compressed foundation hand, but with a slope to the letters of about 10° from the vertical as illustrated in fig.1.

When writing in the italic hand, the most important thing is to keep a constant degree of slope throughout the piece of lettering, as words written at different angles look very untidy. As with the previous two alphabets that we worked on, keep the pen at an angle of 30° to the writing lines. If you have difficulty keeping the letters at the same forward angle of slope throughout your lettering, draw in a few diagonal guidelines at intervals across the page to help you, until you have become used to the correct angle. The letters are formed as shown in fig. 2.

This alphabet is a formal italic, which is more regular and rounded than the sharper, and more angular, cursive italic (which will be the subject of the next chapter). The rounded 'a', 'e', 'g' and 'y' are shown here, but the alternative versions used with the compressed foundation hand can also be used with italic.

fig.1. Italic letters are written with a slope about 10° from vertical.

abcdefghi

jklmnopq

rstuvwxyz

fig. 2. Formal italic alphabet.

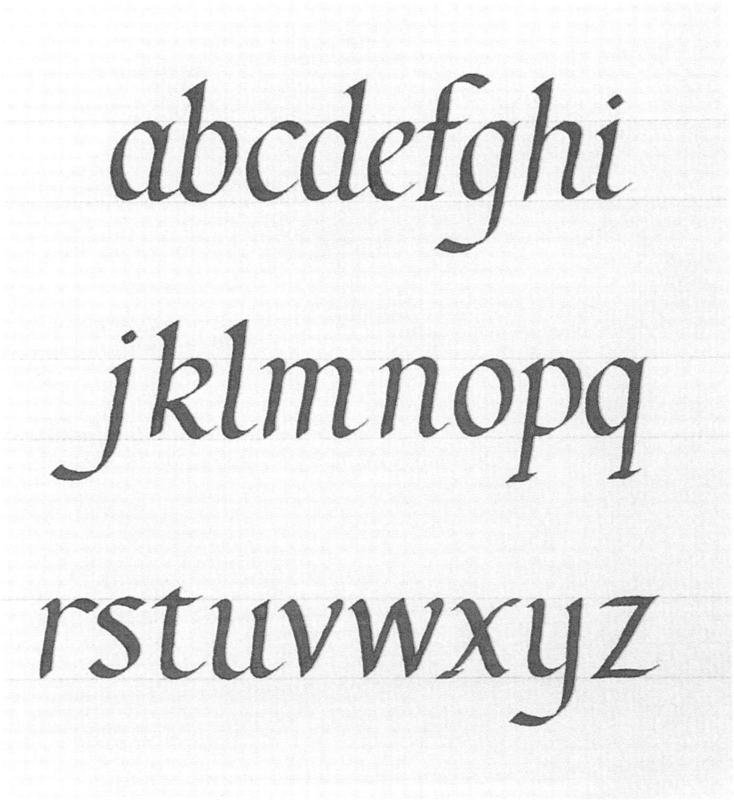

Working with colour

You may need a selection of different colours when you are planning and writing a piece of lettering, such as a menu. Writing with coloured inks can be different from using black ink because the colours are usually of varying consistencies. There are a great many bottled coloured inks on the market, and many are sold as calligraphy ink. As with black ink, the quality varies enormously, but most are generally rather thin and transparent

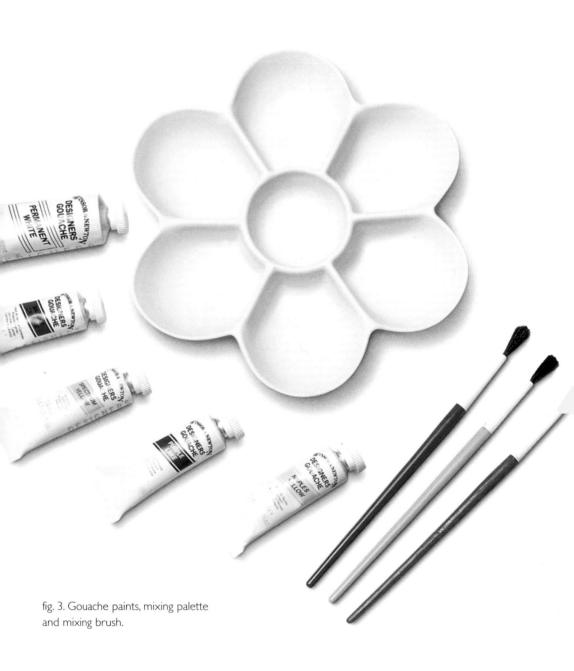

fig. 3. Gouache paints, mixing palette
and mixing brush.

The consistency required for calligraphy is like very thin cream. The paint should be a good, opaque colour, but not too thick to clog the pen. When writing in several different colours, you will find that they vary slightly in consistency. Some colours are quite grainy – the browns tend to be like this – while greens can be difficult to make opaque without the use of a slightly thicker consistency than is required for most other colours. Always practise a few words in any newly mixed colour before working on your final piece of lettering to make sure that the consistency is correct. When working with paint, it is a good idea occasionally to rinse and wipe the nib to make sure that the paint hasn't dried under the reservoir or on the outside edge.

The range of gouache colours is large, because when different gouache colours are mixed together they lose some of their brilliance. You should therefore avoid mixing two or more colours together and instead choose a single colour from the range. All colours have their advantages and disadvantages, so your choice will usually be a compromise when selecting the best one for your work. Some of the most useful colours are listed.

Gouache paint

Scarlet lake is the best red by far: it is a lovely, strong, bright colour, and when it is mixed with water its opacity and consistency are very good. Because it tends to smudge when you are rubbing out any writing lines across which it has been written, when mixing it with water it is a good idea to add a drop or two of gum arabic to make sure that the paint remains firmly attached to the page.

Permanent green middle is a good, medium-coloured green (there are also dark and light versions of this colour). Although greens are inclined to fade when they are exposed to sunlight, this colour lasts better than most of the others. It tends to be transparent when it is mixed to the correct consistency, in which case you could add a little white to it, but remember to be sparing with the white, because the paler the shade of green the more prone to fading it becomes.

Rose Tyrien is a shocking-pink colour that you may find useful on occasions.

Spectrum yellow is a bright, deep yellow, whose strength should be sufficient if you are writing on a pale-coloured surface. If necessary, you could add white to it to make it more opaque, but if you do so try to use as little as possible, because white has a heavier consistency than most other colours and the paint will not flow smoothly from your pen if you use too much. (Writing with white paint is not recommended.)

Ultramarine is a strong, bright blue. Although its colour is extremely vibrant when it is used straight from the tube, it tends to be a little transparent when mixed to the correct consistency. If this happens, add a little permanent white to give it greater opacity.

Burnt Umber is a soft, donkey-brown colour. It is quite dark when used straight from the tube and therefore usually needs a little white added to it. Because this is another colour that tends to fade quickly, however, keep the shade as deep as possible when mixing.

Purple lake is an attractive colour to choose when you need purple – Parma Violet is another good choice. Of the two, purple lake – a reddish-purple colour – does not fade in the light as quickly, whereas Parma violet, which is on the blue side of the colour spectrum, is more opaque.

Chinese ink

Chinese ink sticks are also available in various colours (fig. 4), although these are not as widely available as bottled inks and gouache paints. Grind coloured ink sticks with water in an ink slate (fig. 5) in the same way as black ink sticks until you have obtained the correct consistency and depth of colour.

fig. 5. Coloured ink sticks are ground on an ink slate in the same way as a black ink stick.

fig. 4. (Opposite). Coloured Chinese ink sticks.

Making a menu

The menu should be no larger than A4 (298 × 211mm) size, which is a standard paper size from which printed copies can easily be made. You will need three different sizes of nib: one for the title, one for the name of each course and one for the details of the food.

When designing the menu, begin by roughly drawing out the wording in the order and general shape in which you intend it to appear (Step 1). This will give you an idea of the spacing required for the quantity of lettering to be included.

Work out if your chosen sizes will fit the overall dimensions that you have decided upon for the menu. If you are using a size 4 nib for the body of the text, the line height will be 4mm (⁵⁄₃₂"), with 8mm (¹¹⁄₃₂") between each set of writing lines. Determine if this will enable you to fit all of your text into the size of paper that you intend to use by measuring out the writing lines down the length of the draft sheet. You will find that a size 4 nib will produce lettering that takes up too much space to fit the required menu size comfortably. You should therefore try a size 5 nib for the small-sized lettering.

Enough of a margin needs to be left around the edges to make a reasonable border, as well as for the holly-leaf decoration in the corners (Step 2). Using the line-height guide (which was explained in the previous chapter), try to guess the nib sizes that may be suitable for the other two sizes of lettering that you will be using.

Start by working on the smallest lettering and write out one of the sections in rough to see how it will look (Step 3).

Now work out which size will be best for the course headings (Step 4). The first lettering is too large, so use the smaller size (Step 5). Make a draft of all of the lettering for the courses to check that everything will fit on your paper.

Work out the lettering size for the title (Step 6). It is worth writing the title in several sizes and then cutting them out and trying each in turn. Now add a border (Step 7).

Step 1. Initial sketch of menu contents.

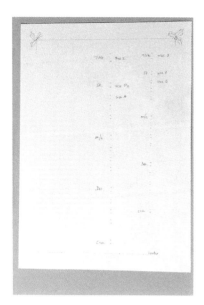

Step 2. To ascertain whether your chosen nib sizes will fit the page mark off the writing lines down the length of a sheet. The column of marks to the left allow for a size 4 nib for the small text but this leaves too little room for the border. The column to the right is measured for a size 5 nib and this will leave plenty of room for the border.

Step 3. Write out and position the small text roughly into place on the layout sheet.

Once you have decided on and drafted all of the lettering to size, rule up your paper or card with the writing lines. Some very attractive papers are available in large sheets or pads of different colours, and a selection is shown in Step 8. An attractive, fairly thick, but lightly textured, paper has been chosen for the menu (Steps 9 & 10). Measure and rule your guidelines and marking points onto your chosen paper. Now you are ready to write your menu card (Step 11). Write the title in scarlet lake gouache. Using a guard sheet, write in all of the course headings in permanent green middle gouache. Add the smaller details in black ink. Use touches of gold paint for the corner decoration and the lines between courses. FInally carefully rub out the writing lines,

Main Course

Main Course

Step 5. The chosen size positioned on the draft.

Step 6. Try the title in a choice of sizes.

Step 7. Add the border to complete the draft.

MENU

To Start

Melon balls with cinnamon
or
Smoked salmon with salad garnish

Main Course
Duckling a l'orange or Roast Lamb with mint sauce
served with new potatoes, green beans and
Julienne of celery and carrots

Dessert
Profiteroles with chocolate sauce
Lemon Meringue Pie and cream
Cheese and Biscuits

Coffee and mints

Step 8. A selection of papers and cards: Constellation Pearl card in satin and shantung patterns; Conqueror laid card in green, pink and blue; Parchmarque paper in white and four colours; Canford card, three colours from an extensive range: Ingres pastel paper in a pad of three colours.

Step 9. The chosen paper is cream coloured Parchmarque card, the surface is quite textured but smooth enough for lettering.

Step 10. The texture of the paper is clearly visible.

MENU

To Start

Melon balls with cinnamon
or
Smoked salmon with salad garnish

Main Course

Step 11. Writing your menu.

MENU

To Start

Melon balls with cinnamon
or
Smoked salmon with salad garnish

Main Course

Duckling a l'orange or Roast Lamb with mint sauce
served with new potatoes, green beans and
Julienne of celery and carrots

Dessert

Profiteroles with chocolate sauce
Lemon Meringue Pie and cream
Cheese and biscuits

Coffee and Mints

Designing a certificate

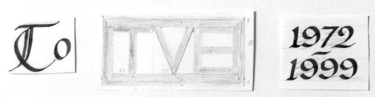

1 | Cut-and-paste draft lettering to determine the arrangement of the landscape layout.

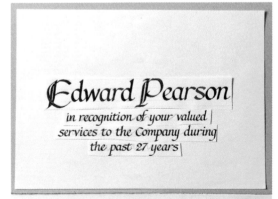

2 Begin the draft with the main title then centralise the smaller text below.

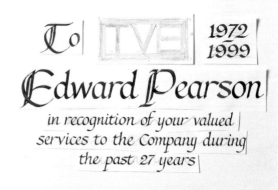

3 Adjustments can be made to the lettering sizes to determine the best combination. Next, the logo, dates and 'To' are arranged in positions that give the best overall balance.

4 This shows the completed draft.

5 The paper chosen for this certificate has a mottled, marble effect and is called Marlmarque. The writing lines are lightly ruled to avoid making indentations in the paper. Add marking points for the start and finish of each line of text. Now you are ready to write your certificate.

A size 1 nib is used for writing the main name and a size 2½ for the three lines of text below. The other words are written with a size 1½ nib. The large initial letters in the main name and 'To' are large italic letters written with double pen strokes for the downstroke of each letter. The same size 1 nib is used, even though the letter height exceeds the usual seven nib widths for capital letters; this is because double strokes make the letters larger and extend them below the bottom writing line. They have each been adapted from other lettering styles to add a little more interest to the design, which, for an A4-sized certificate, contains quite a small amount of text. (Double-stroke letters are covered in more detail in the next chapter.)

The positions of the two large, gold letters can be ascertained by using the draft as a guide. These are written first.

The black text is written next, so that it falls correctly into place after the gold initials.

'To' and the dates are now written, and then finally the lines of text at the bottom. After the text has been completed, the logo is sketched or traced into position. The background colours are now painted. The green and gold lettering and logo are painted in gouache colours.

The outline of the logo is drawn, using a ruling pen for precision.

Finally, the writing lines are removed, care being taken not to smudge the lettering.

To **TVE** 1972 – 1999

Edward Pearson

in recognition of your valued
services to the Company during
the past 27 years

4

Cursive italic

Change of Address:~

From 26 October 2000

Sarah and Chris Eames

will be living at

Telephone
01716 214188

24 High
Milton
Bu

fig, 1. Connecting strokes for cursive italic letters.

fig. 2. Letters 'a' and 'n' in cursive and formal italic. Cursive is on the left.

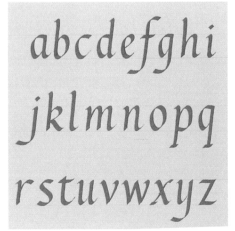

fig. 5. Minimal serifs are used for cursive italic letters.

fig. 4. Rounded letters are written with flattened out top strokes.

fig. 6. Simple cursive italic capitals.

Calligraphy

Cursive italic

Cursive italic, in which there is more of a contrast between the thick and thin strokes, is a more stylish version of the italic hand than formal italic. Cursive italic can be adapted to form a handwriting style that is quick enough to be practical yet still retains characteristics of the more formal calligraphy styles.

*B*efore attempting the whole alphabet, practise the strokes illustrated in fig. 1. These are the two connecting strokes that make this style markedly different from formal italic (compare the two types in fig. 2). Cursive-italic lettering can also be written with more continuous stokes than formal italic.

The whole alphabet is illustrated in fig. 3. Notice that the tops of some of the rounded letters have been flattened out slightly (fig. 4). The serifs, especially the tops of the ascending strokes, are much sparer than those used with formal-italic letters. Most are just a subtle rounding-off of the stroke at its beginning and end (fig. 5), which both aids the speed of writing and makes the style simpler and clearer. The 'f' is usually given a long tail with a bottom stroke to match the 'g', 'j' and 'y'. When a more decorative style is required, this is a lettering style that really lends itself to extravagant flourishes and elongated serifs. (These will be dealt with later in the chapter.)

A set of simple, unadorned capitals that match cursive-italic minuscules are illustrated in fig. 6. Like the minuscules, they have been constructed with minimal serifs and fewer lifts of the pen. They are quite plain, modern-looking letters, which have a very distinctive feeling of flow and movement. These have been used in the piece pictured in fig. 7, which is the text of a passage from Shakespeare's Romeo and Juliet, giving the speeches of each in turn in two alternating colours. (The text is written on blue Conqueror card, which has a laid surface. This card is smooth enough for calligraphy that is written with a fairly small nib, and it also takes ink very well.) Fig. 8 shows a few alternate versions of the cursive italic capitals.

fig. 8. Some alternate cursive Italic capitals.

Writing change-of-address cards

When you are designing a piece of text, you will not always want to centre all of the lettering, and when you are planning a piece whose lettering is off-centre it is important to achieve a good balance of lettering and spacing across the whole page. This is illustrated by the following simple project – a change-of-address card – whose text is shown in draft form in Step 1. The nib sizes used for this piece were a size 3 for the main name, a size 4 for the top line of lettering and a size 5 for the remaining words.

Sketch out a few alternative layouts to see which looks the most attractive (Step 2). The first example, the straightforward, centralised layout, is neat, but rather uninteresting. The second example shows a gradual shifting of the lines of text across the page, from top left to bottom right, with the telephone number fitted into the empty bottom left-hand corner. Vertical layouts are not very practical for this type of card, as the names of people and places need to be split between too many lines to allow ease of reading. The best choice for this piece of lettering is example (b), which has a landscape layout with the text gradually stepping down from left to right.

Make a draft of all of the lettering (Step 3), using the appropriate nib sizes. Cut out the words and arrange them on a layout sheet, making alterations as necessary until you are satisfied with your complete draft.

Measure and rule your guidelines and marking points onto your chosen card. You are now ready to write your change-of-address card (Step 4).

Using a ruling pen, add linear fillers to the two empty corners to balance up the design. The finished card, which was written on peach-coloured Parchmarque card, has a matching envelope.

Change of Address

from 26 October 2000
Sarah and Christopher Eames
will be living at
24 High Bank Cottages
Milton Lane, Westcott, Bucks.
Tel: 01716 214188

Step 1. Text required for a
change-of-address card.

Step 2. A set of alternate sketched layouts for
the change-of-address text.

Step 3. Cut and paste the
text into the chosen layout.

Change of Address :—

From 26 October 2000

Sarah and Christopher
Eames

will be living at

Telephone
01716 214188

24 High Bank Cottage
Milton Lane, Westcott,
Buckinghamshire

Step 4. Lettering your change
of address card.

Change of Address:~

From 26 October 2000

Sarah and Christopher
Eames

will be living at

Telephone
01716 214188

24 High Bank Cottage,
Milton Lane, Westcott,
Buckinghamshire

Fig. 9 shows an alternative design for a change-of-address card. The text has been written diagonally, in black ink and mauve gouache, across lilac-coloured Canford card (Canford is sold in a huge range of colours and is available from many art shops).

fig. 9. A diagonally arranged change-of-address card on mauve Canford card.

Flags and flourishes

Cursive italic can be sharpened to an even greater extent than the examples shown so far, and fig. 10 shows letters which have very acute curves to the beginning and end of their strokes, as well as thin, hairline strokes connecting the main changes of pen direction. Note that the tails of the letter 'p' have been given a backward serif to indicate an increased sense of movement (fig. 11).

As was previously mentioned, cursive letters lend themselves to exaggerated serifs and flourishes. Fig. 12 shows some of the minuscule letters to which it is particularly easy to give this treatment. They are all letters with an ascending or descending stroke that can be given a 'flag' serif to accentuate the forward-flowing movement of the lettering style. Combinations of letters can also be linked to good effect (fig. 13).

Capital letters written in this style are even more adaptable to flourishes, and the alphabet shown in fig. 14 illustrates the letters with several variations of flourished strokes.

fig. 10. Cursive italic letters sharpened further to give greater contrast between strokes.

sharpened

fig.11. The serif on the leter P flows into the down stroke from behind.

fig.12. Flag serifs on ascenders and descenders.

fig.13. Combinations of letters can be linked together.

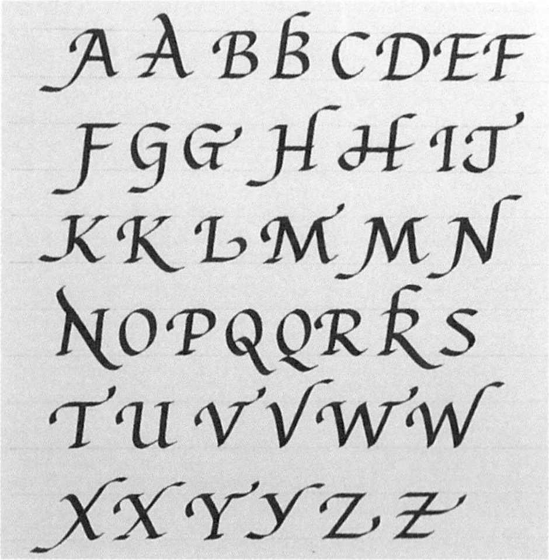

A A B B C D E F
F G G H H I J
K K L M M N
N O P Q Q R R S
T U V V W W
X X Y Y Z Z

fig.14. Flourished italic capitals.

*H*airline serifs are sometimes added to the extremities of cursive italic letters to give an added touch of finesse. You need to be fairly adept with your pen to create a good effect with these, however. A very slight flick of the pen is all that is needed (fig.15), so that only the left corner of the nib remains briefly in contact with the paper. Note that this type of stroke should be a casual embellishment and not a studied addition (fig.16) to the letters, as this destroys their charm and spontaneity.

Fig.15. Hairline serifs. (left)

Fig.16. Over-worked serifs.

Monograms

You can design a monogram by building up a capital letter with a series of flourishes. The best way in which to go about designing it is first to work it out in pencil. Remember that it takes a while to achieve a good design that has smooth, flowing curves and an interesting shape.

Try to keep most of the flourishes on the outside of the letter, which will make it easier to see the letter itself – the design's raison d'être, after all. The 'A' in Step 1 (overleaf) has a simple series of loops at its top and bottom, which curve around and back over themselves several times before ending in a final curl.

Make sure that the design is balanced by ruling a dividing line vertically through the centre of the letter and keeping a balance of pattern on both sides (Step 2). Now trace your design onto your card (Step 3).

Step 1. An 'A' monogram.

Step 2. A dividing line is used on the pencil draft to help balance the design.

Step 3. The letter is traced onto the card giving pencil guidelines to follow when making the flourishes.

Step 4. Take care with the thin diagonal strokes which are the most difficult to produce.

*O*nce you are happy with your pencil outline, work out the best way of making the pen strokes to achieve the best effect. Keep the pen angle the same as when writing ordinary letters, so that you produce the same contrasting thick-and-thin strokes. If you find that some of the strokes are a little difficult to form, such as the long, thin, diagonal strokes from right to left (Step 4), adjust the design to limit these as much as possible.

You cannot make the whole flourish with a single pen stroke, because a metal nib does not work properly when it is dragged backwards for the thin strokes. Each part of the flourish should therefore be a separate stroke (Step 5) which join up perfectly around the curves (Step 6).

Step 5. Each part of the flourish should be a separate stroke.

Step 6. The separate strokes should join up perfectly.

The letter can either be made double-stroked to give an interesting effect or consist of a combination of single and double strokes, which makes a letter look larger and bolder as its limbs appear wider, being composed as they are of two strokes and the space in between. The 'N' shown in fig. 17 has double strokes for each of the three strokes forming the actual letter and curving terminations at each corner. Fig. 18 shows a double stroked 'H' monogram.

With more complex designs, you may find that when you draw in some of the thicker pen strokes the design can look a little congested in the areas where several strokes cross over each other (Fig. 19). Such strokes can also close up some of the gaps, thereby completely spoiling the design. These areas therefore need to be adjusted so that the strokes are more evenly spaced on the final design (Fig. 20).

Two letters give even more scope for creating scrollwork with which to link the letters (Fig. 21 and Fig. 22). Use a smooth piece of paper or card for this work to be sure that you will be able to make the strokes in a flowing, graceful manner. After you have worked out the design, either go straight ahead and try writing it freehand or use a pencil outline as a guide.

Fig. 17. An 'N' monogram composed of double strokes.

Fig. 18. A double stroke 'H' monogram.

Fig.19. This 'Q' monogram has areas where the cross strokes are too congested.

Fig. 20. The redesigned 'Q' monogram now has better spaced crossing strokes.

Fig. 21. 'LC' monogram.

Fig. 22. 'PG' monogram with double stroke letters.

Double-stroke letters

Double-stroke letters can be useful for titles or the initial letters of verses, and an alphabet consisting of double-stroke capitals is shown in fig. 23. An alphabet of double-stroke italic capitals is shown in fig. 24. Although these letters were written with a size 3 nib to a height of 32mm (1¼"), you have a lot of latitude when constructing letters in this manner. For example, the same-sized nib also made the letters illustrated in fig. 25, showing that it is possible to work to a given size and space in order to fill it to best advantage.

A few of the letters have been broken down in fig. 26, and the order in which the strokes were made has been given to help you to master their construction. You will need to practise some of the letters a great deal before you write them, in order to get used to the correct order of stroke construction that is needed to form the best shape. As you can see, double-stroke letters work equally well when they are either upright or have a cursive, forward slant.

When constructing the letters, ensure that where combinations of strokes meet you work them into each other carefully so that you do not end up with an unattractive jumble of lines that meet incorrectly. The letter 'A' is one of the more difficult to construct as a double-stroke letter, because the lines cross in several places.

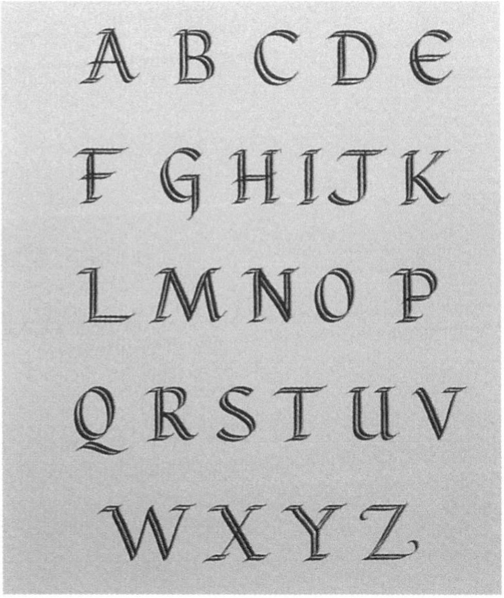

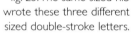

fig. 23. An alphabet of upright double-stroke
capitals.

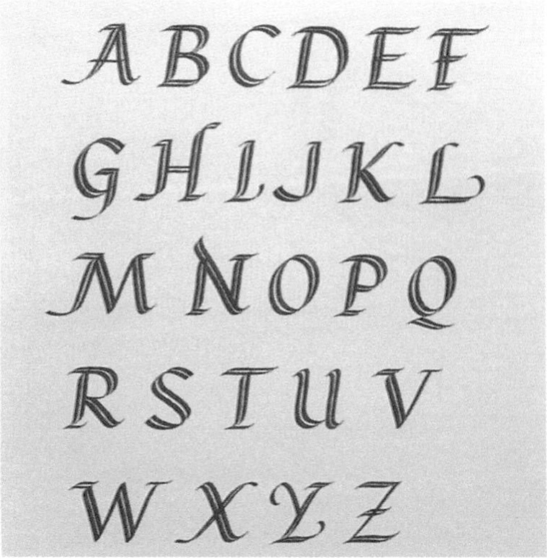

fig. 24. Double-stroke italic capitals.

fig. 25. The same sized nib
wrote these three different
sized double-stroke letters.

fig. 26. The order in which the strokes are
made needs to be worked out and
followed carefully.

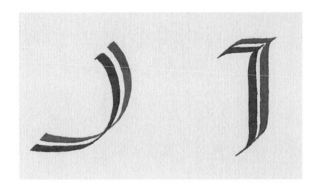

fig. 27. Take care to join up inner and outer strokes correctly.

*F*or letters with curved strokes, such as 'B', 'C', 'D' and so on, the outer curve should be written first, so that the shape is correctly established before the inner curve is added. Where the horizontal strokes running across the bottom of a letter meet the curved strokes, the outer curved stroke should join the top horizontal stroke and the inner curved stroke the bottom horizontal stroke (fig. 27).

Many of the letters, such as 'V' and 'W', look better if one or more of the strokes are left as a single stroke. Others, such as 'L' and 'Y', benefit from the addition of a balancing stroke to maintain an even distribution of weight across the letter.

Fig. 28 is a piece of lettering in which double-stroke initials begin each of the verses, as well as the title. The title letters have been given a more decorative treatment by means of a few additional flourishes. The letter 'H', in particular, lends itself to this sort of treatment.

With regard to the layout of this piece, note that the verses have been offset to the left and right down the page, thereby giving greater width to the whole design. A piece such as this, which has five verses with quite short lines, makes rather a long, narrow column running down the page if the verses are written directly beneath each other. This design spaces the larger initials within the block of text better. The sets of four lines of each verse have given the same treatment by means of stepping alternate lines in and out of each other at the same interval.

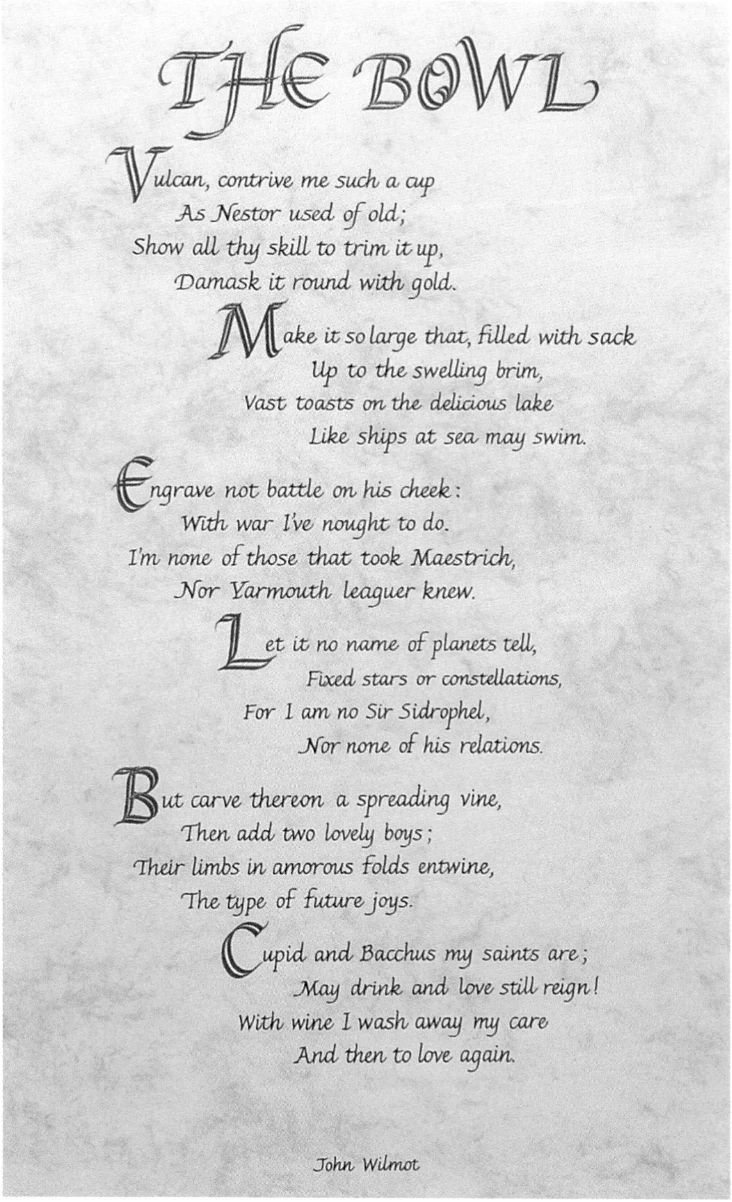

THE BOWL

Vulcan, contrive me such a cup
As Nestor used of old;
Show all thy skill to trim it up,
Damask it round with gold.

Make it so large that, filled with sack
Up to the swelling brim,
Vast toasts on the delicious lake
Like ships at sea may swim.

Engrave not battle on his cheek:
With war I've nought to do.
I'm none of those that took Maestrich,
Nor Yarmouth leaguer knew.

Let it no name of planets tell,
Fixed stars or constellations,
For I am no Sir Sidrophel,
Nor none of his relations.

But carve thereon a spreading vine,
Then add two lovely boys;
Their limbs in amorous folds entwine,
The type of future joys.

Cupid and Bacchus my saints are;
May drink and love still reign!
With wine I wash away my care
And then to love again.

John Wilmot

fig. 28. Text with double-stroke capitals.

*D*ouble-stroke letters are also useful for large-sized lettering, because the double-width stroke forms a letter that is a lot larger than the single-stroke capital when written with a nib. Making double-stroke letters can also enable you to avoid working with very wide nibs, which are sometimes a little awkward to use or may produce inaccurate lettering if the nib is not sharp enough or if it contains too much ink. If you do not want your double-stroke letters to be too large in comparison to the rest of the single-stroked lettering, however, you will need to use a smaller-sized nib.

You can buy pens with points of varying distances and thicknesses (fig.29) that make a double stroke for you. The points are usually quite fine, with the result that the letters that they produce are lightweight, with a transparent appearance (fig.30). The example shown was written with a nib-size 50 Mitchell 'Scroll Writer'. A music pen is also available (fig.31), which has five points for drawing musical staves; of the five strokes produced, the top and bottom strokes are slightly broader than the central three. Such pens are fun to experiment with, and you can also achieve some interesting effects with them.

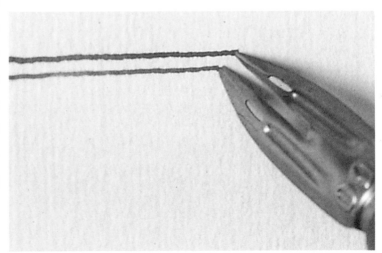

fig. 29. A double-stroke nib.

fig. 30. Letters produced by a double-stroke nib.

fig. 31. A five-line music stave nib.

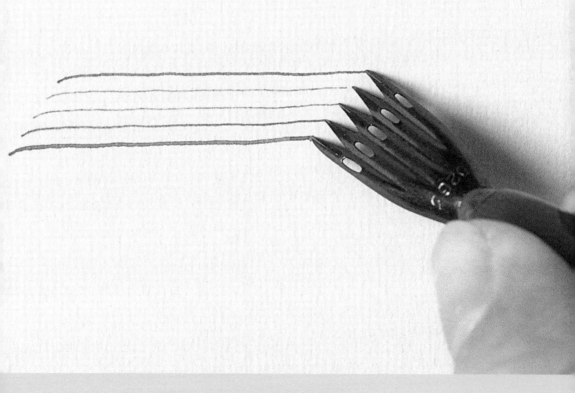

Elswood Horticultural Society

SPRING

FETE

and Plant Sale

Saturday 15th May 2000

ELSWOOD VILLAGE HALL

from 1pm – 5pm

Admission £1

Gardening Advice   Books   Cake Stall   Tombolla   Refreshments   Craftwork   Paintings   Animal Welfare

5

Using capitals

Using capitals

Calligraphy is often needed when writing posters, and we will
deal with some poster projects in this chapter. We will tackle
layout further and also look more closely at large capital letters,
in particular Roman capitals, which were originally quite complex
in construction, but can today be adapted to form a simpler,
modern style.

Roman capitals

Fig. I displays the alphabet of Roman capital letters, while in fig. 2 they are grouped into their different widths. From these examples we can see that the 'O' is completely circular, the 'C', 'D', 'G' and 'Q'
are also based on a circle, while the 'H', 'M', 'N' and 'W' are the full width of the 'O'.

Fig. 3 shows the narrow letters, which are just over half the width of the 'O'. Note the economi-
cal use of fairly small, straight serifs. The remaining letters are shown in fig. 4. In the Roman-capital-
letter alphabet, many of the letters that began with a serif in the alphabets that we previously learned
instead begin with a continuous, straight, vertical stroke downwards (fig. 5), which is followed by a top
stroke that forms the serifed portion. The letters 'B', 'D', 'E', 'F', 'P' and 'R' have received this treatment,
which is similar to the straight–serifed alphabet, but has slightly different proportions to the letters.
The difference between Roman and foundation-hand capitals is that the foundation-hand letters are
all of fairly equal proportions, allowing for their different shapes, whereas the Roman letters are either distinctly wide or narrow, depending on their letter shape.

The Romans were very precise and mathematical in the lettering techniques that they used for
forming inscriptions on monuments, and they constructed their letter shapes so that they balanced
well. Although the same degree of precision cannot be attained with pen-written lettering, the general proportions can be adapted to good effect for work in which clarity and impact are important,
such as posters.

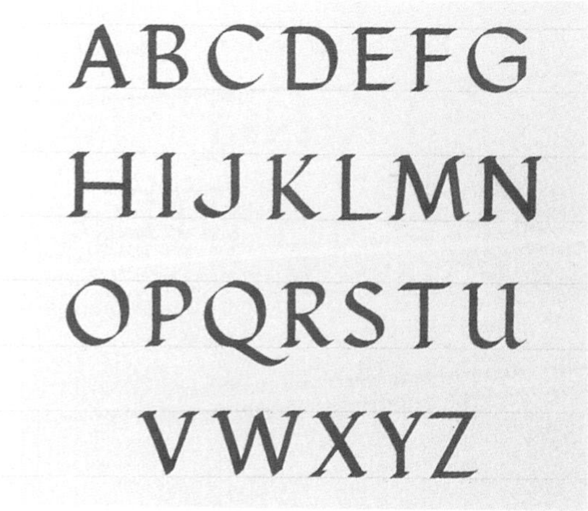

ABCDEFG
HIJKLMN
OPQRSTU
VWXYZ

fig. 1. Roman capital letters.

CDGHMN
OQW

fig. 2. Wide letters.

BEFKLP
RSY

fig. 3. Narrow letters.

ATUVXZ

fig. 4. The remaining letters which fall between the two widths.

fig. 5. Strokes forming the top part of many of the Roman capitals.

Step 1. Five sketches for a poster for a Spring fête.

Step 2. The cut-and-pasted poster DRAFT.

Step 3. Using three measured points to draw diagonal writing lines.

Step 4. Writing the poster.

Working on poster layouts and designs

*O*f the five preliminary sketches for the layout of the spring-fête poster (step 1), layout (b) has been chosen as having the best balance and clarity. It has a bold title and a little floral decoration in the spaces to the right and left of the words, and although the diagonally written words in the bottom portion are easy to read, they do not detract from the more important lettering.

Taking the alternative layouts in turn, the layout of option (a) is a fairly straightforward arrangement, with nothing particularly eye-catching about the design. In addition, the main title, which runs across the top of the page, has less impact than the same words in the other four arrangements. Running on the list of words in the bottom portion in a continuous row, separated only by commas, makes the text a little more difficult to read quickly and is also a rather static design. Choice (c) is made quite interesting by writing the smaller details around the edge of the poster, but this reduces the space available in the centre for the more important text, which would have greater impact if it was larger. Although layout (d) is an attractive design, its different lettering angles make it a little too fussy. As is demonstrated by example (e), a landscape arrangement is not very practical for posters, because the majority of the places in which they will be displayed, such as in shop windows or on trees and noticeboards, suit a portrait-shaped poster better.

Step 2 shows the cut-and-pasted draft of the text for the preferred layout. The capital letters that make up the words 'SPRING FETE' can be given special treatment, and we will use Roman capitals written with a size 3 Automatic pen (see page 96).

The remainder of the description of the event, along with its date, place and time, will be written in compressed foundation hand. The title across the top of the poster will also be in compressed foundation hand, and you should make sure that the lettering is of a size that will enable you to fit all of the words on one line. The venue will be given prominence by means of widely spaced Roman capitals, while the remaining details at the bottom of the poster will be written in italic to introduce a little variety. This means that three different lettering styles will be used for the text, and because any more would create a discordant appearance, this is about the maximum number of styles that you should include on one page.

When ruling the writing lines for the diagonal words at the bottom of the poster, make sure that you keep them parallel by turning the page and marking the measurements accurately. If you do not have a parallel ruler, draw the first diagonal at the correct angle and mark off the other lines from this, using three sets of points per line (Step 3) to ensure that they are accurate.

Measure and rule your guidelines and marking points onto your chosen paper and write your poster, following the draft (Step 4).

Calligraphy

Alternative poster

Another set of information for a poster advertising a craft fair has been cut and pasted into position in Step 1 (overleaf). The main title is in italic letters written with an automatic pen (Step 2). Roman letters spell out the venue details and the contents list at the base of the page, while two further sizes of italic have been used for the rest of the text. Remember that small calligraphic fillers are useful for breaking up areas of text, and two very simple, linear motifs have been added to this layout to separate some of the central details. The finished poster pictured has text written in black ink on a bright-lemon-yellow card.

Printers usually offer a good range of colours for posters, but if you want a specific type of paper – perhaps with a mottled effect or a laid texture – you can buy your own from a specialist paper shop and ask the printers to use that. However, remember that this is only worth doing if you can hang some of the posters where they will be closely scrutinised. Because most posters will usually only be seen from a distance, using a subtly textured or coloured type of paper may be a wasted effort.

Step 1. A cut-and-pasted DRAFT for a poster advertising a Craft fair.

Step 2. Lettering the poster.

Poster and automatic nibs

For posters, your lettering sizes will probably have to be larger than usual. The William Mitchell nibs that we have been using up to this point go up to a size 0, which makes a stroke that is just over 3mm (about ⅛") in width, giving a capital-letter height of about 22mm (about ⅞"). If you need to produce letters that are larger than this, you could buy a set of poster nibs (fig. 6), to each of which a large reservoir is attached that holds the increased amount of ink required. You will have to take care not to overfill the nib, otherwise you will produce blotchy letters and lose the fine lines that are integral to good calligraphic letters. Hiro Leonardt also makes large-sized nibs (fig. 7), whose reservoirs are positioned above, rather than below, the nib.

Automatic pens (fig. 8) are excellent for poster-writing, as they are not only sold in very large sizes, but are also easy to use. Their construction includes two angled pieces of metal with touching edges and a series of small slits along one edge that allows the ink to flow better.

fig. 6. Poster nibs.

fig. 7. Hiro Leonardt nib.

fig. 8. Automatic pens.

When working, make sure that the slitted edge is facing away from the page as you write. Although these pens can be dipped into a container of ink, some of their nibs are so large that they have to be filled with a large, well-loaded brush in order to transfer the ink to the whole of the inside edge. (Be extremely careful when you are moving a fully loaded pen from the inkpot to the paper, although once you are holding the pen at the correct angle to the paper and are ready to write the danger of spilling the ink is past.)

For the craft-fair poster, a number 3 automatic pen was used to write the title. The width of the stroke is nearly 5mm (about ¼"), giving a letter height of 25mm (about 1"). The pen decoration was also written with this pen size.

Writing signs

If you need to work on a very large scale – if you are making a sign, for example – you have two options regarding pens. Firstly you could make your own pen.

Making your own poster pens

Here we are using a piece of absorbent material cut with a thin edge. The example shown is a piece of cardboard with a small piece of cotton fabric wrapped around the end that is held in place with staples. It is rigid enough to provide a good edge for the lettering and the cloth absorbs enough ink or paint to make the letters.

2 Mix plenty of ink, because when you are making large letters with a very absorbent nib you will get through it very quickly. Refill the nib frequently in order to avoid a dry brush effect.

3 The sign illustrated was written with this type of writing instrument on an interesting, Japanese paper flecked with tiny, metallic squares. The width of the stroke made is 40mm (just over 1½") so letters of 200mm (just under 8") could be written if necessary. This lettering has a height of 175mm (nearly 7").

Cork is another good nib-forming material, and a cork from a wine bottle should be long enough for your purposes. You will need a very sharp knife to cut it into shape and remember to take care when cutting, because the cork is quite rubbery and can be difficult to cut. The completed cork nib is quite robust, however. Start by making a straight cut downwards into the cork.

2 Then cut across it to remove a portion.

3 Now scallop off the back edge to leave a thin edge of cork.

Making a cork nib

4 The shape so far should look as shown here.

5 Scallop off side portions to make the end of the nib the required width then shave it down until it is about 1mm (less than ¹⁄₁₆") thick, so that it will give accuracy to your letters.

6 If the writing edge is not straight, make a downward cut along its length. Your nib can also be reshaped if it becomes blunt. (This is more or less the same method that was used to make reed pens centuries ago.)

$\mathcal{T}$he 'RAFFLE' sign (fig. 9) shown was written with a cork nib 19mm (about ¾") wide, and the letters were written between guidelines 90mm (about 3½") high. You will need a small tray of ink, so that when you are dipping the cork pen into it the ink is transferred along the whole of the writing edge. Although you will have to dip the pen into the tray many times – and should be careful to avoid ink drips – the letters can be formed fairly easily, with a good degree of accuracy.

Your second option is to make compound letters, which are letters whose individual strokes are composed with more than one thickness of nib. Compound letters are often drawn first and then written and painted. Being very clear and well-defined, Roman characters – which are often constructed as compound letters – are eminently suitable for signs. The lettering for the sign pictured in fig. 10 was first drawn and then outlined with a size 3 automatic pen before finally being filled in with a paintbrush. This procedure gives a nice calligraphic quality to the letters, as well as retaining the accuracy that can be lost when using large, home-made nibs.

Waterproof signs

If a waterproof sign is required, use acrylic paint, which is mixed with water but becomes waterproof when it is dry. Although the paint is quite thick, which means that the letters will not have the accuracy of gouache-painted characters, a little crudeness is not very noticeable in large-scale letters. Indeed, the overall effect can be very good (fig. 11). If the sign needs to be freestanding, use mount board, which is sold in large sheets and in a wide range of colours by most art shops and picture-framers.

fig. 9. RAFFLE sign written with a cork nib.

CAKES

fig. 10. CAKES sign in Roman letters.

fig. 11. Sign using waterproof acrylic paint.

TEA ROOM

fig. 12. TEA ROOMS sign using a size 6 Automatic pen.

fig. 13. Transparent letters produced with ink that is too thin.

fig. 14. EXIT sign using a size 6a Automatic pen.

The 'TEA ROOM' sign pictured in fig.12 was written with a size 6 automatic pen. Even a pen of this size can produce lines that are very accurate. Unfortunately, the amount of ink that is required for each stroke often necessitates refilling the nib halfway down a stroke, so take care that you rejoin the line very accurately.

When you are using slightly transparent inks or paints, a dark-and-light effect can be produced where a stroke has been stopped and restarted, as can be seen on the letters in fig.13. In order to reduce the chance of this happening, it is therefore best to stick to either black or very dark colours.

The size 6 automatic pen makes a stroke 19mm (about ¾") wide, so capital letters written at the usual seven nib widths would be 133mm (about 5¼") high. Remember that letters on posters tend to look better when they are a little squatter than normal-sized lettering. Six nib widths have there-fore been used for this sign, resulting in better-proportioned letters.

The 'EXIT' sign in fig.14 was written with a size 6a automatic pen, whose nib is about 25mm (about 1") wide. The lettering is 150mm (nearly 6") high, which makes for quite a large sign – this one meas-ures 210 x 750mm (8¼ x 29½"). Although the quality of the letter edges starts to diminish with this size of nib, it is not enough to mar the lettering when viewed from the intended distance.

Rock Buns

4oz self-raising flour
2oz butter
2oz sugar
1 egg
2oz dried fruit

6

Blackletter

Blackletter

Blackletter – another Gothic lettering style dating from the Middle Ages – derives its name from the density of its upright strokes, the closer spacing of its letters and the closer placing of its writing lines, all of which give it a much blacker appearance on the page than the more open styles that preceded it. This type of lettering accompanied many of the beautifully decorated and illuminated books of the medieval period. Although it was also used in some of the earliest printed books, it quickly lost ground to styles that were both easier to read and more practical for the printer to use.

fig. 1. Blackletter practice strokes.

*B*egin learning this lettering style by practising the strokes shown in fig. 1. Because there are not many curved strokes in the blackletter hand, it suits calligraphers who have difficulty making uniformly rounded strokes, although care must be taken to get the spacing right so that the lettering does not look ugly.

The minuscule letters are illustrated in fig. 2. Closely examine the construction of these letters and note that there are several terminations to the upright strokes and that each has a diagonal stroke attached to the beginning and end that is one of three different lengths (fig. 3). As with the other alphabets, the 'm' (fig. 4) is a good example because it uses all three of these strokes in one letter. The first and last strokes are the short diagonal running straight into, or out of, the upright (fig. 3). The bottom stroke of each of the first two uprights must be the small, centrally placed stroke illustrated in fig. 3b; if you do not use this stroke you will close up the gaps between the uprights and make the letter difficult to read. The top two strokes connecting the three uprights are the slightly longer diagonal line that flows out of, or into, the upright (fig. 3c). If you take care when forming these connecting strokes, the style will look even and well balanced.

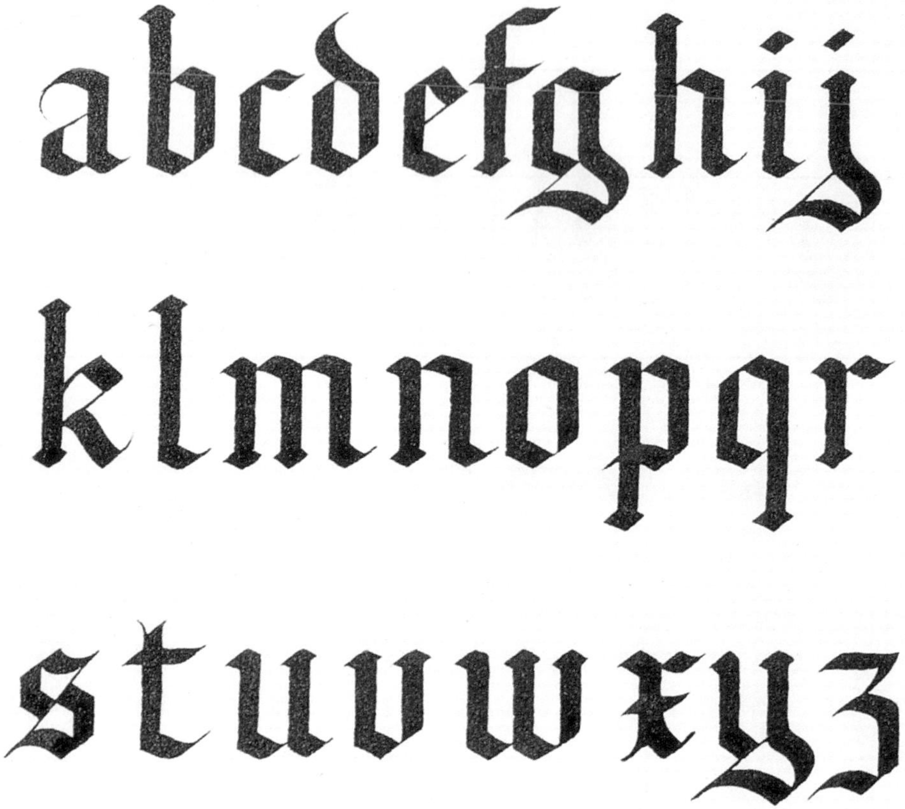

abcdefghij

klmnopqr

stuvwxyz

fig. 2. Blackletter minuscule alphabet.

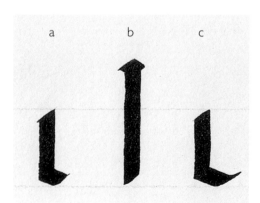

fig. 3. Terminations to upright strokes.

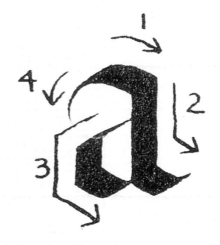

fig. 4. The blackletter 'm' contains the three different terminations to the upright strokes.

fig. 5. Formation of letter 'a'.

fig. 6. Letter 'e'.

The 's' is quite a difficult letter to write because it is formed by changing the pen direction many times (fig. 7). The main strokes are then bisected by a thin, diagonal line running through the centre, which should leave two tiny gaps on either side of the two middle strokes. You will have to adjust your pen very slightly when filling these. The 'x', which is formed as shown in fig. 8, has two central strokes that overlap each other.

Because the letters are written quite close together, and because so many of the strokes are the same, this style can be quite difficult to read. Some of the letters have variants (a few are shown in fig. 9), however, whose use can make the hand both easier to read and more decorative. The final strokes of such letters as 'h', 'n' and 'm' can be given an elongated, curving finish, for example, which breaks up a long row of uprights very well (fig. 10). Similar curves, albeit at the top of the letters, can be added to the 'v' and 'w'. You can find examples of all of these strokes in medieval manuscripts. A crosspiece can also be given to the central strokes of the 'w' and 'm' to make the letters a little clearer. The capital letters of the blackletter alphabet are among the most decorative of any calligraphic hand (fig. 11). As well as being quite complex, there are several versions of some letters – indeed, you can even embellish them further with extra strokes to suit your purposes. Nearly all of them have a thin, vertical stroke placed alongside an upright, and in order to make the thinnest possible stroke you will have to turn your pen completely sideways (fig. 12). A small, extra stroke is often placed within the more open letters (fig. 13). Because these letters are so decorative, however, words that consist solely of capitals are very difficult to read and tend to look overly fussy. If you are using the blackletter hand for titles, it is therefore much better to combine the upper and lower cases instead, and to make the letters' increased size the dominant feature (fig. 14).

The ascenders and descenders of the blackletter style can be given a very attractive finish by means of the fishtail, or Fraktur, serif shown in fig. 15. The serif requires the same sort of hairline stroke that was used in the formation of cursive italic letters, which is made by using the corner of the pen to flick out the extra stroke (fig. 16).

fig. 7. Letter 's'.

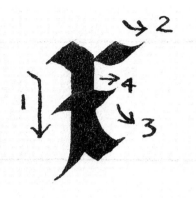

fig. 8. Letter 'x'.

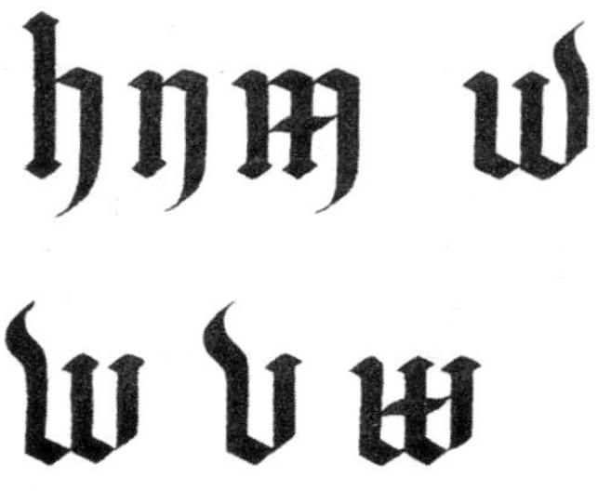

ħ ŋ ɱ ɯ

ɯ ʋ ɯ

fig. 9. Alternate letters.

fig. 10. Using the more embellished letters to improve the legibility of a long row of vertical strokes.

minimum

minimum

ABCDEF

GHJJKLM

NOPQRST

UVWXYZ

fig.11. Blackletter capitals.

fig.12. The pen is held vertically for the
thin strokes of the capital letters.

fig.13. A small additional stroke is often placed within the curved area for decoration.

fig.14. A title in a mixture of blackletter minuscules and capitals is much easier to read than one composed of capitals only.

Ye Olde Tea Shoppe

YE OLDE TEA SHOPPE

fig.15. Fraktur serifs.

fig.16. The serif needs a deft manipulation of the corner of the nib.

Making a calendar

$\mathcal{N}$umbers can be written to match the straight-sided, blackletter style, and these are shown in Step 1. Because they are not very easy to read, however, it is generally better to accompany most lettering styles with the simpler numerals of one of the plainer styles, for example, when you are writing an address, for which legibility is very important.

A simple, calligraphic calendar can be made using a heavy weight of paper or thin card. Write out the names of the seven days of the week in fairly large lettering (the examples shown in Step 2 were written with a nib size of 1). Write the months of the year in the same size, too, but in a different colour. Leave plenty of space between each word because the cards will all be cut to the same size. Cut the cards so that each word is central (Step 3).

Write the numbers 1 to 31 with a larger nib (for the numbers illustrated in Step 4 a size 3 automatic pen was used, making figures 30mm (about 1") high).

Cut out all of the pieces of card to a height of 60mm (2 6⁄16"). The cards containing the weekday and month names should be cut to a width of 120mm (4 3⁄4") and the numerals cards to a width of 60mm (2 6⁄16").

You can display the day's date in various ways. Firstly, you could make a central hole at the top of each card and then hang the cards on a row of hooks fixed to a small board. You can buy suitable hooks from a hardware shop. Secondly, you could make a simple stand out of thick folded card, fashioning a lip at the bottom to hold the cards (Step 5)

A third alternative is to fix the cards into place on a board with strips of Velcro. Velcro (usually black or white), which is available from haberdashery shops, is composed of two strips of fabric that adhere to each other, but that can be pulled apart time and time again. Buy the 'stick-and-stick' version, which is adhesive on the back of both strips, so that one piece can be applied to the back of a card and the other to the board (Step 6). If you look at the Velcro closely, you will see that one side is composed of tiny hooks and the other of a mesh of loops, to which the hooks catch. Use pieces of the hooked side of the strip for the cards and of the looped side for the display board. The board can then be hung up (Step 7).

Manufacturers of commercial display boards often cover them with a fabric that is designed for Velcro attachments, and you may be able to find such display boards and boxes of small, circular, Velcro fasteners in office-supply shops.

01234 56789

Step 1. Blackletter numbers.

Step 2. Write the weekdays and months in a large lettering size.

Step 3. The weekdays and months are centralised on the cut cards.

Step 4. The numbers 1 to 31 are written in foundation hand for clarity.

Step 5. A simple stand for the calendar cards is made from thick folded card.

Step 6. 'Stick and stick' Velcro.

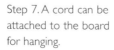

Step 7. A cord can be attached to the board for hanging.

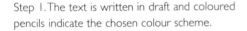

Shall I compare thee to a summer's day?
Thou art more lovely and more temperate:
Rough winds do shake the darling buds of May,
And summer's lease hath all too short a date:
Sometime too hot the eye of heaven shines,
And often in his gold complexion dimm'd:
And every fair from fair sometime declines,
By chance, or nature's changing course untrimm'd;
But thy eternal summer shall not fade,
Nor lose possession of that fair thou ow'st,
Nor shall death brag thou wander'st in his shade,
When in eternal lines to time thou grow'st;
So long as men can breathe, or eyes can see,
So long lives this, and this gives life to thee.

Shakespeare

Step 1. The text is written in draft and coloured pencils indicate the chosen colour scheme.

Step 2. Rule up the writing lines then, using a central vertical line for measuring, mark the start and finish points of each line of text.

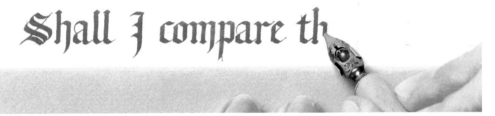

Step 3. Proceed with the lettering.

calm was the day,
and through the

Step 4. Blackletter needs only one letter height between each pair of writing lines.

A Shakespeare sonnet

Because the blackletter hand is very dense, a piece of text written in a block in this style looks very effective. The Shakespeare sonnet shown in Step 1 consists of lines of roughly the same length and therefore lends itself to this treatment.

Cutting and pasting text can be avoided with a layout like this because the lines are so similar in length that writing them out, line after line, as a straightforward practice piece will provide you with enough guidance for the final work and will also give you a good impression of how the finished piece will look in terms of its density of text, line spacing and so on.

When you have written the draft text, measure the length of the lines (Step 2) to help you to make small adjustments to the starting point of each line to ensure that all of the lines are centred when you are writing the final piece. Any lines of text that are a little shorter than the majority can be indented slightly, making the difference in length less noticeable, while those that are slightly longer can be started slightly further forward to give a square block of text. Now write out the text (Step 3). Because blackletter is written with only one letter height between each line of text, take care that you do not make the ascenders and descenders too long (Step 4).

Shall I compare thee to a summer's day?
Thou art more lovely and more temperate:
Rough winds do shake the darling buds of May,
And summer's lease hath all too short a date:
Sometime too hot the eye of heaven shines,
And often in his gold complexion dimm'd:
And every fair from fair sometime declines,
By chance, or nature's changing course untrimm'd;
But thy eternal summer shall not fade,
Nor lose possession of that fair thou ow'st,
Nor shall death brag thou wander'st in his shade,
When in eternal lines to time thou grow'st;
So long as men can breathe, or eyes can see,
So long lives this, and this gives life to thee.

Shakespeare

Making borders

*I*t is important to give some thought to the borders that will surround your work. Some examples are shown in fig.17. If you leave too little space for a border, the text will look as though it has been crammed onto the page. By contrast, if the borders are too large, the text may look a little lost. Good border proportions are usually achieved by allowing about a quarter of the width of the block of text for the side and top borders. The bottom border is generally made a little wider to give a balanced appearance.

Another Shakespeare sonnet is illustrated in fig.18. The initial letter has been enlarged for decorative purposes. If you allow a large initial letter to extend beyond the rest of the block of text, you could add a simple, coloured, floral-patterned border down the left-hand edge (fig.19). By allowing the initial letter to protrude beyond the top line of the text you also can work the border along the top edge of the design, as well as down the left-hand side. By slightly shifting the block of text in relation to the page you can furthermore either extend the border around three sides or make it completely surround the text.

You can also introduce small motifs and decorations to pieces that consist of several verses by placing these between the verses (fig. 20 and fig. 21). Alternatively, you could write the text within any suitable shape (fig. 22). A framed piece is illustrated in fig. 23.

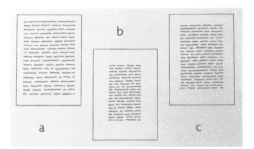

fig.17. Different border widths. (a) too narrow
(b) too wide (c) correct.

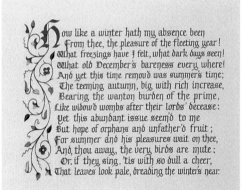

fig.18. Sonnet.

fig.19. Border construction.

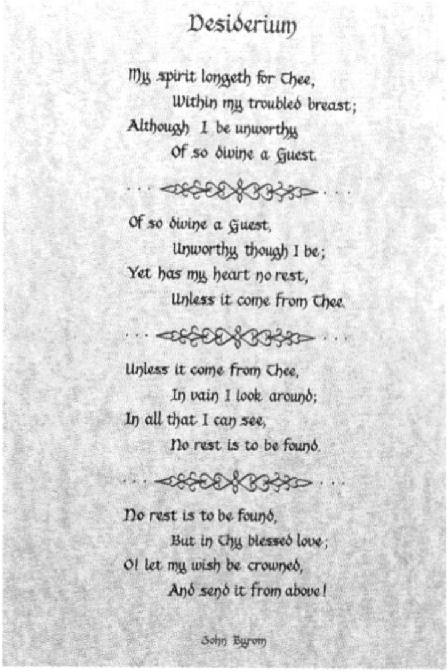

Against Idleness and Mischief

How doth the little busy Bee	How skilfully she builds her Cell!
Improve each shining Hour;	How neat she spreads the Wax!
And gather Honey all the Day	And labours hard to store it well
From ev'ry op'ning Flow'r!	With the sweet Food she makes.

In Works of Labour or of Skill	In Books, or Work, or healthful Play,
I would be busy too:	Let my first Years be past,
For Satan finds some Mischief still	That I may give for every Day
For idle Hands to do.	Some good Account at last.

Isaac Watts

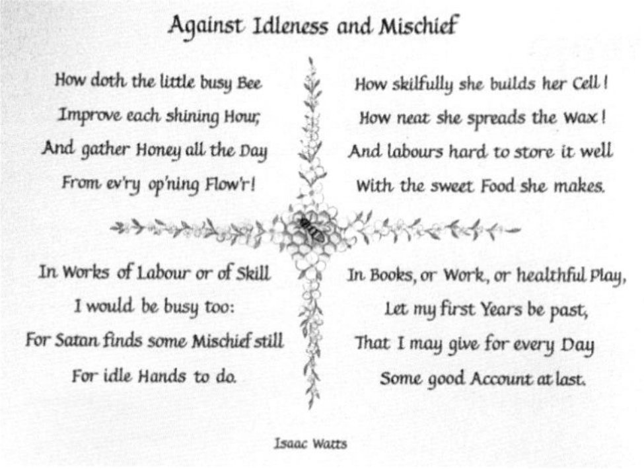

fig. 21. The verses can be arranged around a central decoration.

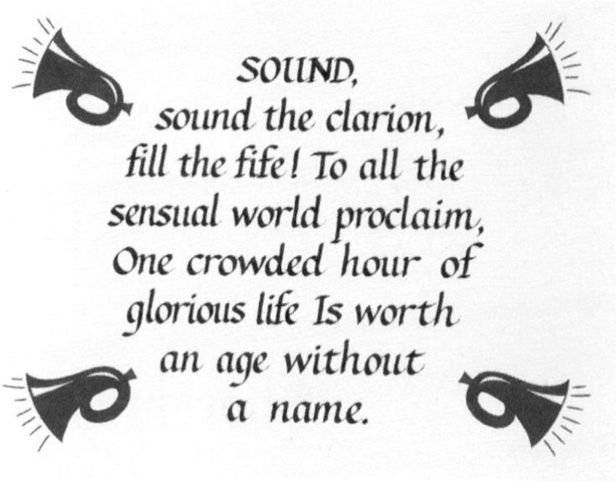

Desiderium

My spirit longeth for Thee,
  Within my troubled breast;
Although I be unworthy
  Of so divine a Guest.

Of so divine a Guest,
  Unworthy though I be;
Yet has my heart no rest,
  Unless it come from Thee.

Unless it come from Thee,
  In vain I look around;
In all that I can see,
  No rest is to be found.

No rest is to be found,
  But in Thy blessed love;
O! let my wish be crowned,
  And send it from above!

John Byrom

fig. 20. Decoration between each verse embellishes this text.

SOUND,
sound the clarion,
fill the fife! To all the
sensual world proclaim,
One crowded hour of
glorious life Is worth
an age without
a name.

fig. 22. The text of this piece has been fitted into a circle.

fig. 23. Two columns of text are separated by a central illustration.

Rock Buns

4 oz self-raising flour
2 oz butter
2 oz sugar
1 egg
2 oz dried fruit

Rub fat into flour then add sugar and half of the egg then the dried fruit. Mix all together and place in spoonfuls on a greased baking tray. Cook for 15 minutes in oven Reg. 4

Step 1. Here the title is centred, with ingredients to the left and method to the right.

Macaroons

2 egg whites
5 oz castor sugar
5 oz ground almonds

few drops almond essence
almonds or cherries
rice paper

Whisk egg white until very stiff. Add almond essence, then sugar and ground almonds. Roll the mixture into rounds and place - well spaced out - on rice paper. Put a cherry or almond on top of each biscuit. Bake for 20 minutes at Reg.4 When nearly cold, remove from tin and tear around the rice paper.

Step 2. Here the ingredients are split into two columns, with a centred title and the method the width of both columns.

Shortbread

1 oz castor sugar
2 oz butter
3 oz plain flour

Preheat oven to Reg.4. Cream butter until very soft. Add sugar and cream until light and fluffy. Stir in flour in very small amounts. Press mixture into a tin. Cook for 20 minutes. Dredge with castor sugar while still hot.

Step 3. The title and ingredients are on the left, with the method on the right.

Calligraphy

Constructing a recipe book

*T*he final project in this chapter is a recipe book, some of whose recipes have been written in draft. The title and list of ingredients for each recipe have been written in blackletter, while the cooking method is in italic.

If you want to create greater visual interest by varying the layout of the recipes from page to page, you could position blocks of text in ways that suit the quantity of text contained in each recipe. Step 1, for example, starts with a straightforward, centred title and then lists the ingredients in a block to the left, with the method being written on the right.

In Step 2 the ingredients have been split into two columns below the centred title, with the method occupying the entire width of both columns beneath them.

Because the list of ingredients illustrated in Step 3 is short, it has been placed under the title on the left-hand side of the page, with the method written in a block on the right to balance it.

Step 4 shows a long list of ingredients centred down the page, with the method split into two columns to the left and right of them. The book can contain even more variants – to arrive at a good layout, regard the lettering as blocks of text that can be moved about the page and split into further blocks if necessary. This method of designing a page of text is useful for many types of work.

When you have decided on your layout, measure and rule the guidelines and marking points on your paper, and proceed with the lettering (Step 5).

The recipe book itself could either be a pre-bound book containing good-quality paper, or you could instead make and bind a simple book yourself. If you are making your own recipe book, first cut sheets of paper to form double-page spreads, allowing generous margins so that you can accommodate larger areas of text if necessary.

When you have a large enough collection of recipes (for example, six double-page spreads) to make a volume, bind them together with a title page and cover. You will need a thick, decorative paper for the cover. Alternatively, you could buy some purpose-made binding paper that has been strengthened with a mesh of fabric.

Constructing a recipe book (continued)

Florentines

Melt sugar and butter in pan. Add fruit, nuts and beaten egg, mix well. Grease baking trays and place teaspoonfuls of mixture, well apart, on these. Cook for 10-15 mins. at top of oven, Reg. 3

4 oz castor sugar
4 oz butter
1 egg
3 oz chopped glacé cherries
3 oz raisins
2 oz chopped walnuts
4 oz plain chocolate

until golden brown. Remove from tray, with a palette knife, when nearly cold. Cool on wire trays. Melt chocolate and spread over one side of each biscuit.
Makes 25-30.

Step 4. The ingredients are centred down the page, with the method split into two columns.

4 oz self-raising flour
2 oz butter
2 oz sugar
1 egg
2 oz dried fruit

Step 5. Proceed with your lettering.

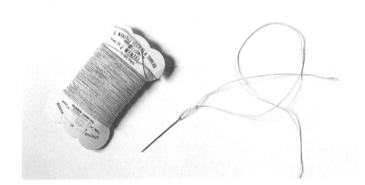

Step 6. A large needle and thick binding thread are needed.

*T*he pages are sewn together using binding thread and a large binding needle (Step 6). Sew them along the central crease through five evenly spaced marks as shown in Step 7. Push the needle through all the sheets each time. (Step 8). Bring the ends of the thread to the centre of the pages and knot them together around the central thread (Step 9).

Step 7. This diagram indicates the direction the sewing thread should take.

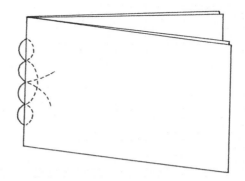

Step 8. Carefully sew the pages together.

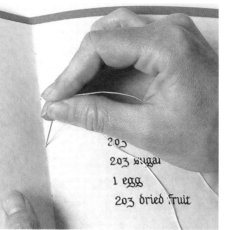

eat oven to Reg. 4. Cream
er until very soft. Add
ur and cream until light
fluffy. Stir in flour in very
ll amounts. Press mixture
a tin. Cook for 20 minutes.
dge with castor sugar
le still hot.

20๖
203 sugar
1 egg
203 dried fruit

Step 9. Knot the ends around the central thread then cut them off leaving about an inch.

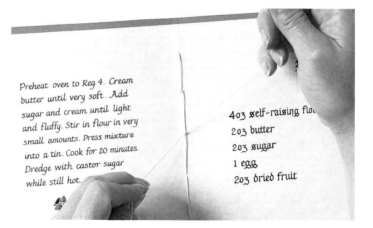

Preheat oven to Reg. 4. Cream
butter until very soft. Add
sugar and cream until light
and fluffy. Stir in flour in very
small amounts. Press mixture
into a tin. Cook for 20 minutes.
Dredge with castor sugar
while still hot.

403 self-raising flo.
203 butter
203 sugar
1 egg
203 dried fruit

7

The uncial hand

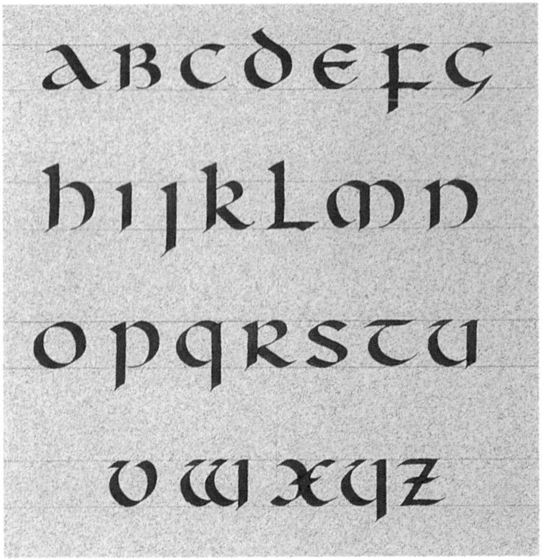

aʙcdeꝼç

hijklᴍn

opqꞃꞅꞇu

ʋꟃxyz

fig. 1. Modern uncial alphabet.

fig. 2. The writing line height for uncials is 4.5 times the width of the nib.

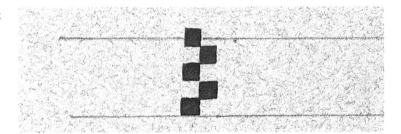

fig. 3. The pen is held at an angle of 20°.

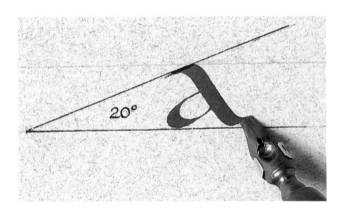

20°

The uncial hand

The uncial letters that can be seen in eighth- to tenth-century Celtic manuscripts have a squat, rounded appearance that can be useful for many types of decorative work. The letters are widely spaced, being closer to the round, or foundation, hand that we learned first than to the compressed styles that we subsequently moved on to.

*T*he letters shown in fig.1 are a simplified and modern form of the original uncial hands that were used during the Dark Ages. Because the letter height is slightly shallower than in most other styles, a height of four-and-a-half times the width of the nib will give a better effect than the normal five (fig. 2). A slightly shallower pen angle is also required (fig. 3).

The ascenders and descenders should be kept very short. In addition, as in the blackletter style, the height between the writing lines should be the height of one letter only (fig. 4). In conjunction with the greater width of the letters, this will result in lettering that takes up a lot of space horizontally, but not vertically, so if you are writing a piece of text that contains a large number of short lines this style will give the piece greater width.

The small, wedge-shaped serif of this hand is very easy to construct. The point that is given to the ascending strokes (fig. 5) is simply a short, diagonal stroke taken to the left, and then to the right, before the downward stroke is begun. At the end of the horizontal stroke, the thickened, terminating stroke to such letters as 'e', 'f' and 'l' is formed in a similar way, that is, by making another short stroke diagonally downwards near to the end and then drawing the nib back up to the end of the horizontal to join the two strokes (fig. 6).

The letter 'a' begins with a diagonal stroke that is curved at each end to follow the natural direction of the pen. The narrow, loop shape that forms the rest of the letter is one continuous stroke that balances the diagonal. The 'b', 'c', 'd' and 'e' are all well-rounded letters. Remember, however, that when you are forming the top stroke of the 'd' you should take care to bring it round to the correct position so that it completes the circle that was begun by its first stroke.

The horizontal bar of the 'f' extends slightly beyond the end of the top stroke, while the descending stroke finishes just below the bottom writing line. The 'g' differs from the 'c' only in having a slight tail at the bottom, which can be made without lifting the pen from the page after making the second rounded stroke. The 'h' is usually given the rounded second stroke that is shown here, and care must be taken not to bring the final, trailing stroke too close to the first upright stroke, otherwise the letter will look like a 'b'.

Although the 'i' and the 'j' were not originally dotted, in order to make the lettering easier to read they can be given a thin, sideways stroke to form a 'dot'. The bottom of each of the aforementioned letters, as well as several others, is given a small serif in the form of another thin, sideways stroke, but in this case it should be less pronounced than that used for the 'dot' – make it

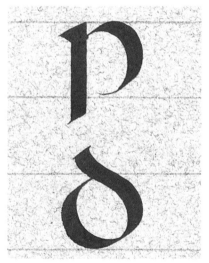

fig. 4. Keep the ascenders and descenders short and allow one letter height between the writing lines.

fig. 5. The small wedge shaped serif given to vertical strokes.

Calligraphy

with little more than a diminishing flick of the pen. The 'k' and the 'r' are the same, apart from the lengthened first stroke of the 'k'. Because the squatness of these two letters can make them look quite cramped, and the looping second stroke and final diagonal are compressed into a small area, make sure that you write them as clearly as possible. The 'l' has a bottom stroke that is the same length as the horizontal stroke of the 'f'.

An 'm' formed with rounded outer strokes and an 'n' with a rounded second stroke have been illustrated here, but remember that there are various alternatives to these two letters (some of which are shown below), any of which may be used in combination in a piece of lettering. When you are writing the rounded 'n', do not take the end of the curved stroke too close to the vertical. A completely circular 'o' is used, while the 'p' is composed of only two strokes, with no extra small stroke joining the vertical to the rounded stroke. The end of the rounded stroke is carried around to meet the vertical, with the corner of the pen finishing the stroke. Although the rounded shape of the 'v' is almost circular, the curve of the second stroke has been modified slightly, so that although there is a gap at the top, the second stroke still meets the first at the bottom in a matching curve that makes the letter look as though it were round.

fig. 6. The thick terminating serif to horizontal strokes on the 'e', 'f' and 'l'.

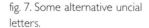

fig. 7. Some alternative uncial letters.

ABCD

fig. 8. Angular capital letters often found accompanying uncials.

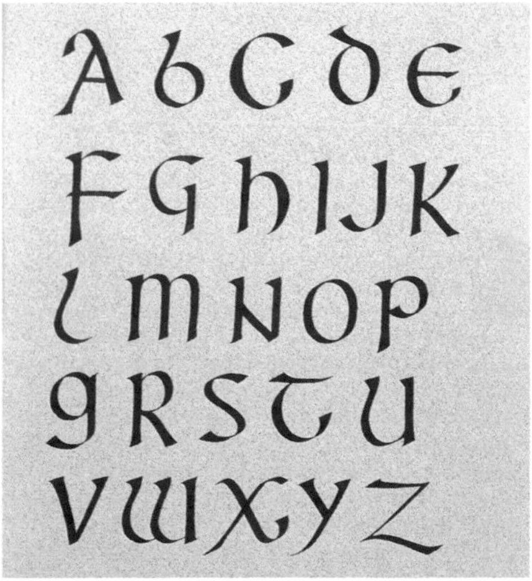

ABCDE FGHIJK LMNOP QRSTU VWXYZ

fig. 9. Large uncials used as capitals.

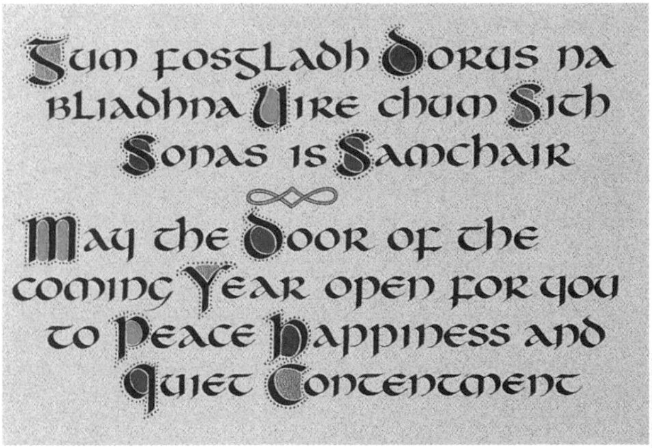

Sum fosgladh dorus na bliadhna Uire chum Sith Sonas is Samchair

May the door of the coming Year open for you to Peace happiness and Quiet Contentment

fig. 10. An Irish text scattered with lightly illuminated letters.

fig. 11. The letter is filled with a colour and surrounded with red dots.

ABCDEFG HIJKLMNO PQRSTUV WXYZ

fig. 12. Eighth century Uncial alphabet.

Alternative uncial letters

Fig. 7 shows some of the alternative uncial letters that can be used in place of those given above. The unusually shaped 'g' is more likely to be encountered in an original uncial alphabet, but because it is not very recognisable in a page of text, you will need to decide whether clarity or authenticity is more important to the particular piece of lettering that you are working on. Note that the 'l' illustrated here has the same curve as that used for first stroke of the 'b' in the letters shown here.

The alternative 'y' is not found in Celtic manuscripts, but is shown here because it can be helpful when you want the text to be very legible (the version given above can closely resemble a 'u' at first glance).

Enlarged miniscules

Uncial text did not contain capital letters at the beginning of sentences. Where it was necessary to place emphasis on particular letters, an enlarged version of the minuscule was used instead, often with a little extra embellishment of colour and decoration. Large, very angular letters can be found in groups in some Celtic manuscripts, and these can be used as capital letters. Because they were usually drawn and painted rather than being written with a pen, however, their shapes do not lend themselves to being written as part of an ordinary block of text (fig. 8).

The enlarged versions of the minuscule letters are made with a nib of the same size as that used for the rest of the text, but are built up with several stokes of the pen to create the extra weight needed for their increased height. If you have trouble with these large-sized letters, work on them on layout paper until you have formed a pleasingly shaped letter. You can then trace the outline of this letter and use the tracing as a guide, either for subsequent letters or for your final pieces, until you have become proficient enough to write them freehand. Fig. 9 shows an alphabet of letters based on Celtic-manuscript uncials that can be used as capitals.

The Irish saying (with its translation) shown in fig. 10 is a typical uncial text, with larger, lightly illuminated letters scattered over the page. The centres of the large letters, as well as the spaces around them, were filled with another colour and then surrounded by red dots (fig. 11). The original uncial letters were written with the pen held at very flat angle (fig. 12). If you look at old manuscripts, however, you will see that it would not have been possible for the scribe strictly to adhere to a constant pen angle when producing some of the strokes, so you can use a little latitude when writing this alphabet. Indeed, there are many variants to some of the letters, which nevertheless retain a Celtic feeling.

Designing a Celtic greeting card

We will now make a greeting card that features the well-known Irish saying Caed Mille Failte ('One-hundred-thousand blessings'). You will need a fairly stiff card of at least 150gsm (grammes per square metre) for this project.

Because you will probably want it to fit into an envelope, the card has been designed with dimensions of 210 x 105mm (around 9 x 4''). Not only are there plenty of envelopes available in this size, but it will also suit the wording very well.

Because the design includes few words, you will need a large-sized nib. Experiment a little until you have found the best size (Step 1). Here, a size 1 1/2 nib was first used, which worked quite well. Since there was still plenty of unfilled space on the card, however, the lettering was then written with a size 1 nib. Not only did the lettering produced also fit within the required space, but it also had a bolder, more striking appearance. The size 1 nib was therefore chosen over the size 1 1/2 (Step 2).

Write out and centre the smaller lettering of the translation (Step 3). A size 4 nib was used here, with the writing lines 4mm (about 3/16'') apart. This size seemed ideal, so no further experimentation was needed.

Now decide on the decoration. In this example, the three initials will be given the simple, filled centre and surround of dots that was mentioned above (Step 4).

Cut the card to size – 210 x 210mm (about 9 x 9'') – and leave it unfolded while you are working on the lettering (it is easier to measure the writing lines accurately from a straight, cut, top edge rather than from a slightly uneven, doubled-over edge).

Work out the position that the text will occupy on the bottom portion of the unfolded card and rule in the writing lines (Step 5).

Write the text and then decorate it (Step 6). (Always leave the decoration until the text has been written in case you make an error that may necessitate you having to start again.)

Fold the card, matching up the corners carefully, and crease it slightly. Use a bone folder to finish the crease, which will give you a crisp, sharp fold. The finished card is shown in Step 7.

Step 1. Choosing the best nib size.

Step 2. Experimenting with an alternative nib.

Step 3. Add the small lettering.

Caed Mille Failte

[one hundred thousand blessings]

Step 4. Add the decoration.

Step 5. Measure and rule the writing lines on the unfolded card.

Calligraphy

Step 6. Use a bone folder to give a crisp fold to the card.

Caed Mille Failte

[one hundred thousand blessings]

Step 7. The finished card.

Celtic decorative motifs

A Celtic new-year greeting-card design is illustrated in fig. 14. (Bliadhna Mhath-ur means 'Happy New Year').

Celtic manuscripts abound in wonderful motifs with which to decorate texts: knotwork patterns interwoven with animals and birds can be used to enliven any piece of lettering, for example, and many good source books feature illustrations from such great Celtic manuscripts as the Book of Kells and the Lindisfarne Gospels.

fig. 14. A New Year
greeting card.

Celtic birthday card

*T*he design for the birthday card pictured in Step 1 was arrived at by first writing the lettering in uncials, using large initial letters for each word. When centred beneath one another on the draft (Step 2), the three words suggested a square, rather than a rectangular, shape for the card, and because the corners were obvious areas to decorate, an outer pattern of Celtic knotwork that concentrated on these areas was decided upon. One corner was first designed using a linear pattern (Step 3), which was repeated in each corner (Step 4), the corners then being joined with twisting bands to form a complete border. The card used was Marlmarque.

Step 1. A Celtic knotwork card.

Step 2. The centred words suggest the overall proportions of the card.

Step 3. Beginning of the linear pattern.

Step 4. The border is a repeat pattern of each corner.

Paper and card for calligraphy

Paper and card for calligraphy need to have various suitable characteristics, the most important being surface texture. Paper that is not porous enough will result in the ink sitting on the surface and not penetrating the fibres properly. Although the ink will dry after some time, the letters are unlikely to be sharp and clear. By contrast, paper that is too porous will cause the ink to spread among the fibres like blotting paper, and crisp, sharp-edged letters will again not be produced. Two very good papers that have just the right degree of absorbency are the Fabriano Ingres and Arches papers (fig. 15). Others that you may be able to find locally are T H Saunders, Waterford and Canson papers. Such papers are usually sold in large sheets, and the Fabriano Ingres and Canson papers come in a wide range of colours (fig. 16), as well as a choice of thicknesses.

Apart from its absorbency, the correct surface texture is also important because some papers can be quite rough, in which case the nib may catch on any loose fibres, resulting in either a spatter of ink across the page or badly formed letters. This is less of a problem when you are using larger nib sizes than those numbering from 3 to 6. Although you can sometimes use a rough texture to your advantage, in that you can produce an interesting effect, a fairly smooth surface is generally preferable.

When you are buying handmade papers, you will find that they are described according to their surface texture. 'Rough' papers have been pressed between sheets of felt before being dried, with the result that the texture of the felt is impressed onto the paper. 'Not' papers are smoother, because the

fig. 15. Some good papers for calligraphy – Arches Aquarelle, Canson Mi-Teintes, Fabriano Ingres, Fabriano 5, Waterford.

fig. 16. A selection of the Canson and Ingres paper colours.

sheets are pressed together several times, while 'hot-pressed' (HP) papers are given a much smoother surface by being pressed between hot metal plates.

When paper is made, a pulp consisting of its fibres is shaken in a large tray until the pulp is evenly spread over the whole surface of the tray. In the case of handmade paper, the fibres end up lying in a more random manner, which gives a less pronounced general direction to the fibres than when they are shaken by machine, which produces less variation in movement. The dominant direction of the fibres will give the paper a more pronounced grain direction when it has dried. This can be seen when a sheet of paper is torn: the tear produced across the grain is far more jagged than a tear made along the grain, that is, in the same direction as the fibres. Remember this when you are cutting paper and card – perhaps for greeting cards – as not only is it is easier to fold, but you will also achieve a neater, sharper crease when folding along the grain rather than against it.

A laid surface can be given to the paper by making it in trays whose wire mesh has a more pronounced pattern. Watermarks are similarly produced, in that the wires are formed into a specific shape. Because fewer fibres lie on the raised parts of the wire's design, a variation in surface texture that corresponds to the shape of the wires is produced when the paper is turned out of the tray.

Paper thickness is measured in grammes per square metre (gsm). The average writing or office-stationery paper weighs between 90 and 110gsm, which is rather thin for calligraphy because it is likely to crinkle when it is dampened by ink and paint. A good weight for most calligraphic lettering is 150gsm. If you require card, you will find that 300gsm is a fairly stiff weight that will stand up on its own.

fig. 17. Vellum effect papers – real vellum, Parchmarque, Pergamenata (vegetable parchment), Elephanthide.

The durability of the paper could be an important factor when you are planning a piece of lettering. If you want to ensure that your paper will not deteriorate too quickly, look for an acid-free, conservation-grade paper. Most good paper shops will be able to tell you the acid content of their papers and advise you on which to choose.

Paper manufacturers have long been trying to produce acceptable substitutes for vellum and parchment, writing surfaces that are very good for lettering. Not only can mistakes be fairly easily removed from these animal skins, but their veining can look very attractive, too. Some of the papers that have been made in an effort to reproduce some, or all, of these qualities are shown in fig. 17. All are very good-quality papers, with different characteristics.

A selection of coloured papers that have different textures and patterns, such as a mottled or marbled effect, are pictured in fig. 18. Japanese paper manufacturers produce some very attractive, decorative papers, some of which are shown in fig. 19. Many are suitable for lettering and can add a lot to your designs. Woodgrain paper, which is available in a large range of colours, has a surface that is perfect for lettering. And although some of the lace- or string-effect papers can be more challenging, they can also be written upon successfully.

fig. 18. Textured and patterned papers: Ingres pastel paper, mottled green; Canson Mi-teintes – mottled dark grey and light grey; Countryside; Kashmir; Marlmarque in a range of colours; Cloud Nine paper in six colours; hammer embossed; linen embossed.

fig. 19. A selection of Japanese papers.

Seating Plan

Top Table

Mr Timothy Dodds
Mrs Patricia Edwards
Mr James Collinson
Mrs Georgina Edwards
Mr Simon Edwards
Mrs Anthea Collinson
Mr Anthony Edwards
Miss Chloe Webb

Table 2

Miss Connie Partridge
Mr Andrew Good
Mrs Pauline Collinson
Mr Reg Collinson
Mrs Sandra Gains
Mr Peter Gains
Miss Helen Gains
Mr Alan Westbrook

Table 3

Miss Sylvia Porritt
Mr Jason Stock
Mrs Lynne Edwards
Mr Norman Edwards
Miss Janine Edwards
Master Ryan Edwards
Master Daniel Edwards
Mrs Edith Edwards

Table 4

Mr David Collinson
Mrs Linda Collinson
Mr Kevin Collinson
Miss Susie Galloway
Mr James Jell
Mrs Lorna Jell
Mr William Collinson
Miss Carla Stenning

Table 5

Mr Gary Markham
Mrs Angela Markham
Mr Jim Lowe
Mrs Tanya Lowe
Miss Dana Lowe
Master Peter Lowe
Mrs June Rawlings
Mr Thomas Gardener

Table 6

Mr George Edwards
Mrs Katherine Trabbett
Mr Brian Wilson
Mrs Gina Wilson
Mr Roger Edwards
Mrs Corinne Edwards
Mr David Banks
Mrs Linda Banks

Table 7

Mr Thomas Collinson
Mrs Wendy Collinson
Mr Simon Collinson
Ms Tina Denning
Mr William Allott
Mrs June Allott
Mr James Allott
Miss Petra Trent

Table 9

Mr Graham Pass
Miss Fiona S
Mr Eas
Miss Lyn
Mr S
Mrs

Mr. + Mrs. James Collinson
request the pleasure of the company of

Mr. + Mrs. G. Markham

at the marriage of their daughter

Georgina
to
Mr. Simon David Edwards

on Saturday 15th July 2000 at 2 pm.
at
St. Andrew's Church, Lamesley

8

Copperplate lettering

Copperplate lettering

The final lettering style that we shall learn is copperplate, which printers usually call palace script, or just script. This is the style that is most commonly associated with invitations and wedding stationery, and is also useful for filling in the blank spaces of a form or certificate that has been printed in copperplate (fig. I). If you need to write on a pre-printed card such as this, make sure that it will take the ink acceptably, as some printed cards can be quite shiny and unabsorbent. When removing any writing lines, be especially careful not to smudge the ink, which may have dried on the surface of the paper without penetrating the fibres sufficiently and could therefore be removed more easily than you expect.

Copperplate was also the hand that was used for writing official documents during the eighteenth, nineteenth and early twentieth centuries, and many old vellum deeds can be seen that are inscribed in beautiful copperplate handwriting. Indeed, certain longstanding establishments still continue to write some of their prestigious documents in this way.

fig. I. Copperplate lettering on a printed certificate.

Copperplate lettering

Of all of the lettering styles, copperplate is the least forgiving of error and needs a great deal of practice to master. The nib required to write this hand is different from the broad-edged nib that we have
used for all of the other styles that we have learned, in that it has a thin point (fig. 2). The William
Mitchell copperplate nib also has an elbow bend to make it easier to use. No reservoir is required,
as quite a few of the letters can be written each time that you dip the nib into the ink. Take care not
to press down on the nib too heavily as you make your strokes, however, or else its fine points will
splay apart and the ink will not flow from it properly.

There is no need for a range of nib sizes for copperplate lettering, because the same nib makes
all of the lettering sizes, as illustrated in fig. 3. As you can see, in the case of the smaller lettering heights,
a difference of half a millimetre in the width of the writing lines can make quite a difference to the
lettering size. The angle of slope of the letters is about 45°, but you can vary the angle to suit your
own preference to a certain extent, the only requirement being that you keep whichever degree of
slope you choose constant throughout the piece of lettering.

MITCHELL
COPPERPLATE

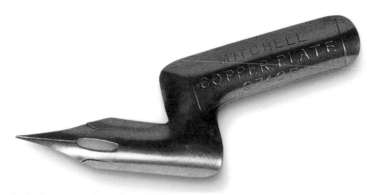

fig. 2. The copperplate nib.

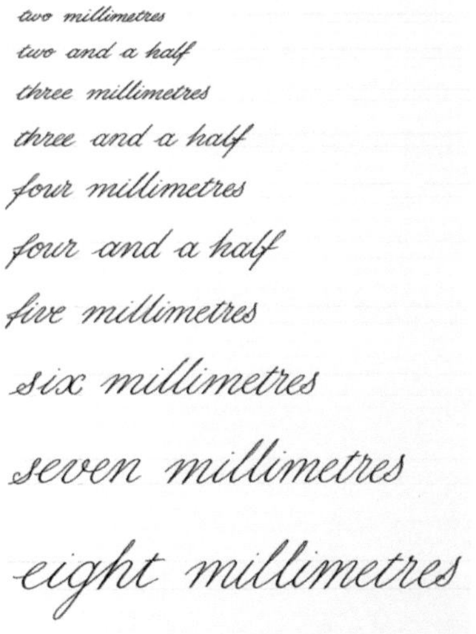
two millimetres
two and a half
three millimetres
three and a half
four millimetres
four and a half
five millimetres
six millimetres
seven millimetres
eight millimetres

fig. 3. Different lettering sizes can be written with the same nib.

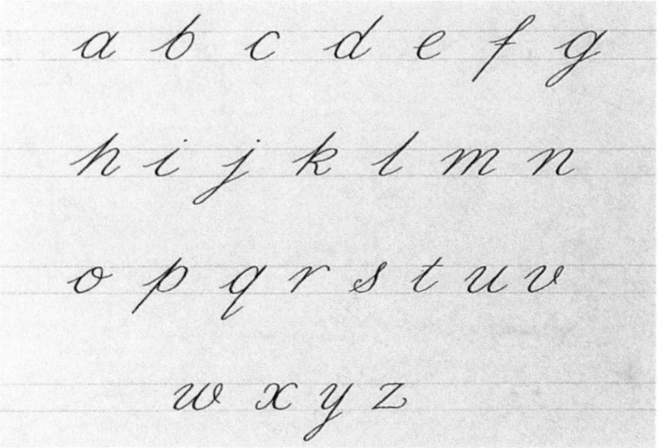
a b c d e f g
h i j k l m n
o p q r s t u v
w x y z

fig. 4. Copperplate minuscules.

The basic copperplate alphabet is shown in fig. 4. The main difficulty that this hand will give you is keeping the constant degree of slope to the words, and if this causes you real problems, use diagonal guidelines, as well as your normal writing lines, to ensure that you keep the angle constant (fig. 5). The height between the writing lines should be at least two letter heights, and three or four letter heights can often look better because the ascending and descending strokes are long, elaborate flourishes (fig. 6).

the flowers of

the

fig. 5. Text with diagonal guidelines behind to help maintain a constant angle of slope to the letters.

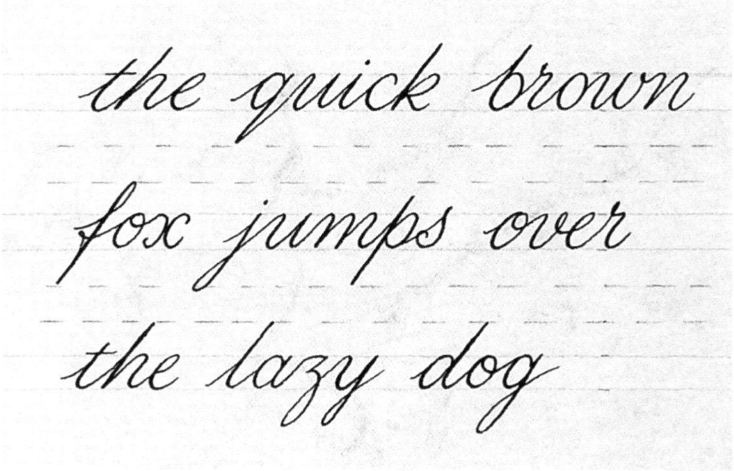

the quick brown

fox jumps over

the lazy dog

fig. 6. Lines of copperplate text with three times the writing line height between each pair of lines.

fig. 7. Squared ends to the ascenders.

fig. 8. Looped ends to the ascenders.

a b c d e f g h

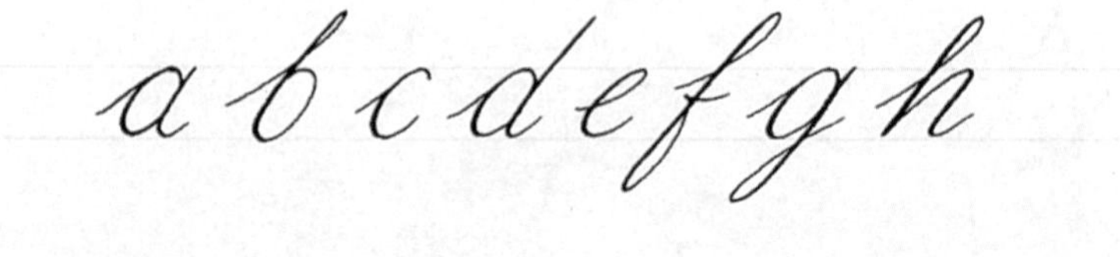

fig. 9. Keep the height of the ascenders contant.

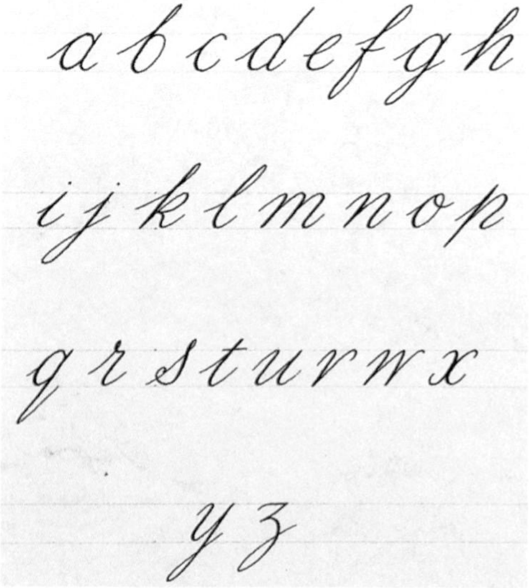

a b c d e f g h

i j k l m n o p

q r s t u r w x

fig. 10. The complete alphabet with looped ascenders and descenders.

y z

$\mathcal{T}$he difference between this style and those that are written with a broad-edged pen is that you form the letters with fewer lifts of the pen from the paper. The nib can be moved backwards where necessary, giving the style an attractive fluidity. Words are written in continuous streams, with only the occasional break being taken to cross or dot letters like 't' or 'i'. Because the nib point is so fine, you will need to write on a fairly smooth-surfaced paper, as one with too much texture will not enable the pen to glide freely over the surface and thus create the hand's long, smoothly flowing strokes.

In their simplest form, the ascending strokes are broad and blunt-ended. Letters never commence from the top of an ascending stroke; instead the pen is first taken upwards in a sweeping stroke from the left, as if it were coming from another letter. Where the pen stops and then begins the downwards stroke, a neat, squared end is made (fig. 7). When you become more proficient in this style, you could try giving the uprights looped ascenders (figs. 8-10). The larger your lettering, the easier it is to produce looped ascenders and descenders, and the more they complement the writing (see the 8mm- (⁵⁄₁₆''-) high letters in fig. 3 (page 204). When making the looped ascenders, the pen stroke from the left sweeps further across, before looping back to make the letter's downstroke.

The linking of copperplate letters is vital if the rhythm and flow of the words are to be maintained. Each letter is linked by a fine stroke leading from the bottom right of the previous letter to the top left of the new letter. Where there is no natural connecting stroke – as with such letters as 'r' and 's', which finish with the pen in the wrong position to start the next letter – a break in the flow is necessitated, the next letter commencing with an initial sweeping stroke from the left (fig. 11). Alternatively, versions of some of the letters (fig. 12) can be formed to include a connecting stroke.

The letter 'f' may cause you problems, as the central crossbar is often formed with a continuous linking stroke leading from the bottom loop to the crossbar (fig. 13). The descender having been formed, the pen either sweeps backwards to run up to the crossbar or forwards to make the bottom loop, before crossing back over the descending stroke to form the crossbar. The 'k' can be given either a looped or straight second stroke (fig. 14). It is also possible to make rounded and curved versions of the 'v' and 'w', while the 'z' has both a normal and a tailed version.

The capital letters for the copperplate hand are shown in fig. 15. Some alternatives are shown in fig. 16. These can be greatly embellished to make them attractive, illuminated letters with which to accompany texts (fig. 17).

fig.11. Connecting strokes for difficult letters.

fig.12. Some letters can be formed differently to incorporate a connecting stroke.

fig.13. Two versions of the letter 'f'.

Calligraphy

fig.14. A few other alternate letters.

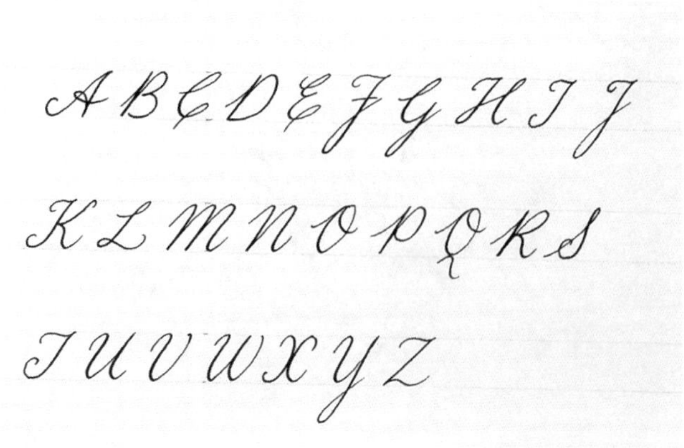

fig.15. The capital letters.

fig.16. Alternative versions of some capitals.

fig.17. Embellished capitals.

Making a wedding-invitation card

When making a wedding-invitation card, first make a rough draft of the lettering to the size and shape required, emphasising the most important lines of text: the names and places (Step 1).

Start by guessing the sizes of lettering that will look best, and then cut and paste the alternative versions until you have achieved the best combination (Step 2).

When you are happy with your draft, measure and rule the guidelines and marked points onto your chosen card and proceed with your lettering (Step 3).

Step 1. Wedding invitation card draft.

Step 2. The cut and pasted draft.

Step 3. Proceed with lettering.

Addressing envelopes

Before addressing envelopes, first make a template so that you won't have to rule a set of writing lines on each. Carefully measure and cut a piece of card to the size of the envelope so that the card fits quite snugly inside it (Step 1). This will prevent the card from shifting slightly and displacing the lines.

Lettering with a height of 3mm (about ⅛'') is about the right size for most envelopes. Six sets of writing lines will suffice for most addresses. Rule up your writing lines on the card, leaving 7mm (about 5⁄16'') between each pair in the central portion of the envelope. Allow a reasonable margin at the top- and left-hand sides.

Step in each line by an equal amount. For smaller, squarer sizes of envelope (Step 2), step in each line by about 5mm (about 3⁄16''). For a longer envelope (Step 3) step in the lines at 10mm (about 7⁄16'') intervals to make better use of the area available.

Rule in the guidelines, making them quite thick so that they will show through the envelope (Step 4).

If an address has only four lines of text, start writing it on the second pair of lines so that the lettering will be more centrally positioned on the envelope (Step 5).

Step 1. Make a template for addressing small envelopes.

Step 2. On a small envelope each address line is stepped in by 5mm.

Step 3. The address lines are stepped in 10mm on longer envelopes.

Step 4. Short addresses should be started at the second pair of lines on the template.

Step 5. The lines should be thick enough to be seen through the envelope.

Making a seating plan

*O*ur next project is a seating plan, which has to be quite large so that several people can see it at once when it is on display. If it needs to be freestanding, write it on mount board, which has a good surface for calligraphy and is available from most art shops in a wide range of colours.

Arrange the tables of guests – 11 in the example shown – on your draft in the same position in which they will be placed in the dining room.

Use a lettering size that will allow you to fit all of the text within the board that you are using. The mount board sold by art shops is usually about 60 x 85cm (about 23¾" x 33⅝") (Step 1), but you may be able to buy larger pieces from picture-framers.

Write the guests' names and the title (Step 2). Given the quantity of guests in this example, lettering 3mm high was needed to fit in all of their names without making the text appear too cramped. The title was written with 10mm high lettering to balance the rest of the text.

Add a simple border (Step 3) to decorate the design. This is made with a ruling pen (Step 4).

Calligraphy

Step 1. Calculate the text size needed for the size of mountboard.

Step 2. Proceed with lettering.

Step 3. A simple border can be added in matching colours.

Step 4. A ruling pen is used for the border.

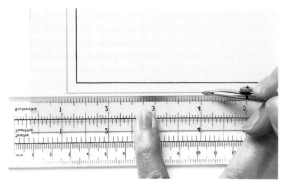

Index

Acknowledgments

The author and publisher would like to thank the following:

Mr Window
for permission to reproduce the large family tree on p160

Mrs Angela Lynskey
for creating the flower display shown on p200